From Fear to Mindful: How to Courageously Transform Your Sales into Lifelong Relationships

First printing July 2023
Library of Congress Cataloging-in-Publication Data

from fear to mindful: how to courageously transform your sales into lifelong relationships / by sam king

Paperback ISBN: 9798398970197
Hardcover ISBN: 9798398970852

Published by AR PRESS, an American Real Publishing Company
Roger L. Brooks, Publisher
roger@incubatemedia.us
americanrealpublishing.com

Edited by Azaile O'Brien
Interior Design by Eva Myrick, MSCP

Printed in the U.S.A.

FOREWORD BY
Brian Tracy

FROM FEAR TO MINDFUL

How to Courageously Transform Your Sales Into Lifelong Relationships

Sam King

The first thing you'll notice is that this book cover is loud and in your face, which is something a salesperson should never be.

This is an extraordinary book, loaded with some of the most important lessons and advice ever discovered. Let the ideas change your life!"

Brian Tracy, Author/Speaker/Consultant

WARNING AND DISCLAIMER!

The methods in this book have been proven in retail settings to help any salesperson or consultant sell more big-ticket items in a competitive commission-based environment. This allows for the strengthening of customer relationships without losing integrity. Other salespeople may be able to use this methodology, but it has not been tried and tested.

You have been warned.

Table of Contents

Introduction

Without sounding arrogant, I've always been reasonably intelligent and always did well in school, provided I wasn't fooling around or doing something I shouldn't be.

My older brother opened a little carpet shop when I was around eleven years old, and from that age onward, I've always been around retail settings.

I started off as the "Saturday Guy," cleaning up, making tea and coffee, and doing other menial tasks. Until one day, when we were driving to work, my brother turned and said to me, "You're serving customers today."

I went absolutely white with shock and could feel my palms begin to sweat.

I've always put on the bravado of being the toughest guy in the room, the life and soul of the party, and acting as if nothing bothered me. In reality, I was just trying to fit in. Experiencing new ventures or putting myself out there has always been scary. When I was learning to swim and I moved up to the big pool, I cried because of how cold and deep the water was! The thought of serving customers terrified me.

My brother's business partner mentored me over the coming months and years and was extremely patient with my progress, even when I made mistakes such as ordering carpets in the wrong colors and sizes, costing the company hundreds, if not thousands, of pounds.

He was a former Royal Marine, and therefore, everything had to be right. He made me stand accountable for my actions, which made me grow and become more efficient at work. Even though I've always had an extremely high work ethic, this added to the meticulous detail that had to be shown.

As you read this book, I hope you'll see that making mistakes was crucial to my success in sales and life in general. It's making mistakes that help us reflect on where we went wrong and what we can do to change and be better in the future. I think we'd all agree that this is the true essence and definition of experience.

After some time, I started to excel in my position, growing in confidence every day and enjoying my role. I could feel that I was becoming an integral part of the business.

I was passionate and enthusiastic. I loved every second of helping customers and having a genuine want and desire to fulfill their needs. When a customer was happy with their choice, it was—and still is—the best feeling in the world.

Sales are a very intimate experience, as we're taking a peek into customers' everyday lives. During sales, subjects are shared that normally wouldn't be in day-to-day conversations, especially with people they've just met. Therefore, it should be treated as an honor that they would be comfortable enough to share with us. This is why we should take customers seriously in order to provide the very best customer service possible.

Having a connection and building a relationship with a customer such that you are almost friends is magical. Not only is this a feel-good factor, but it also helps the bottom line. Customers keep coming back to the company, and they recommend it to their friends and family. As any good businessperson would tell you, this is the cornerstone of success.

I worked with my brother for a number of years until I felt that I had outgrown the company. I then went on to work for a few other retailers selling sofas, couches, beds, dining furniture, and more. This time, commission was involved, and in some cases, they were quite substantial amounts.

This was a completely different ballgame from working with my brother. With him, I was paid a set wage and served customers to the best of my ability because that's just how it was.

I wasn't serving them for my own best interest; I was serving them because they deserved the best possible service as they were spending their hard-earned cash. Sounds like common sense, right? I wasn't ready, however, for what was about to happen next.

I wasn't aware of what other salespeople were prepared to do to get ahold of that money and I stepped into a man's world.

Lying, cheating, stealing, and general underhanded behavior were not in my vocabulary and were the last things to enter my mind. I thought, *How could this happen in a work environment?*

That's the world of sales in any environment, whether it be B2C or B2B. What I realized was that as soon as money becomes involved in any walk of life, people's intentions and behaviors can completely change, and most importantly, I learned not to take it personally.

This is the world of sales, and we definitely aren't going to change it. Therefore, it's our job to adapt and make sure we stay true to ourselves while nurturing sales relationships with customers that last a lifetime and not giving in to short-term gain.

I've always loved the psychology of learning how other people think and what better subject to take an interest in when dealing with hundreds of people a week? I even studied the subject in college before leaving, and when I say leaving, I mean that I actually got kicked out. But that's another story.

At that point in my life, I was relatively young and earning good money. As I was still living at home, my expenditure was at a minimal, so I had a lot of excess cash every month.

Being a young, red-blooded male, I spent a lot of this cash in nightclubs and bars up and down the country and in many cities around Europe. Very often, I would let my emotions get the better of me and enter into activities that, in all honesty, I probably should have stayed clear of. I then came to the realization that if I was to succeed, these behaviors had to be eliminated from my life.

At my peak, I easily surpassed my target without fail and was outperforming salespeople who were "unbeatable."

One of the main reasons I did this was because I wasn't afraid of being myself. No matter where I worked, I always got up every day with the best intentions of giving it my absolute greatest effort and serving customers to the best of my ability, regardless of what others thought of me. Obviously, being in a commission-based environment will create animosity wherever you work. Other salespeople are not going to like somebody coming in and taking their dinner money, especially when they've fallen into a routine or have a food chain where everybody fits in too. I advise you to be that disrupter and ignore the shop floor politics wherever you work without being sleazy, aggressive, or hard-nosed. Your financial and spiritual well-being depend on it. By being your true self and letting your creativity flow, you'll be a better salesperson and provide much better service.

This method proves that it's possible to be a top salesperson without being pushy, negative, or underhanded.

Quite the opposite: it's our positive attributes that will not only make us the best salespeople on the shop floor, but we'll also provide the best service possible, while earning the most commission, of course.

In this book, I'm going to share some secrets and insights with you that I used daily to become the top salesperson, which I have never shared with anyone before!

You'll notice how I never use the word "prospect" to describe people who haven't bought yet. Although technically this may be right, I always use the term "customer." As far as I'm concerned, everybody who walks through the door is a valued customer and needs to be treated as such. Having this mindset was critical to being as successful as I was.

Before we go any further, instead of saying to yourself,

"This doesn't apply to me."

Ask yourself-

"How does this apply to me?"

This shift in mindset opens so many more opportunities to grow.

So that you're aware, I donate a percentage of all proceeds to provide the "Tools of a Salesperson" to children in underprivileged countries. Basically, we provide pens and paper for children to have the right equipment to have an education. We just recently sent our first shipment of stationery to a school in Nepal! So, thank you for buying this book, as this will obviously also go towards the total revenue. The exception is if you bought it on World of Books or a similar website of course, but if you're kind enough to make a donation, then that would be fantastic!

Shall we dive in?

Chapter 1

Fear is defined in the dictionary as an unpleasant emotion or thought that you have when you are frightened or worried by something dangerous, painful, or bad that is happening or might happen.

It is something we all experience. Whether it be a new environment such as a new job or moving to a new city. However, taking these chances and being out of our comfort zone is essential for growth.

Like Dan Pena says, "Fear is **F**alse **E**xpectations **A**ppearing **R**eal."

When we experience fear, it has the capacity to paralyze us. We freeze. Our minds go blank, and we become a deer in the headlights. Have you ever felt that? That crippling anxiety that leaves you scared and unconfident.

We go into "fight or flight" mode. Either we don't act out of fear, wilt in the background, slowly dying, or we overcompensate and become aggressive. While wilting in the background is never a good option in any scenario, neither is becoming overly aggressive.

Let's think about how these behaviors affect our work on the shop floor.

Wilting and going into our shells certainly isn't going to be helpful when serving customers and trying to hit sales quotas. Customers need to trust salespeople enough to give them the benefit of the doubt before handing over their hard-earned money. Would you feel comfortable handing over your cash to somebody who wasn't assertive or confident in themselves?

Probably not. And even if you were, I'm sure there would be a seed of doubt in the back of your mind. As for the other side, would you feel comfortable if somebody was overly aggressive?

You know the type: that alpha salesman who doesn't listen to the customer's needs, the one who shoots down other people, and thinks that they have an absolute divine right to do and say whatever they want on a sales floor. Sure, they may make some sales this way, but what about the havoc they've caused? The toxic culture on the shop floor? The animosity between the staff? And more importantly, what about the relationship with the customer?

Will that customer leave the store happy, having just had a fantastic experience? No. Will they leave with a feeling they'll recommend that salesperson to their friends and family? Probably not.

Even if the product is delivered on time and turns out to be exactly what the salesperson said it would be and fulfills all the customers' needs and wants, a bad taste will be left in the customers' mouths. This can happen just because of the salesperson's behavior and attitude, which can lead the customer to think twice before returning, even if it was just a fleeting thought. These are the exact scenarios that we should avoid in sales. We need customers to instinctively think in a positive manner of a particular person or company as soon as a certain subject is brought up.

The salesperson is the brand of the company. Of course, there are the advertisements that paint a wonderful picture of a store filled with quality products. However, it's ultimately the salesperson who will leave an everlasting impression. They are on the frontlines of the company and the way they interact with people is the most important part.

Imagine you're speaking to a friend, and she needs a new dining set. You purchased a new set a few months ago. It was perfect–everything you could have ever wished for. The service was fantastic, and the salesperson, Leanne, was a dream to deal with.

Without hesitation, you'd mention to your friend how good your experience was. It's an instinct to recommend the company you worked with and maybe even mention how great Leanne was serving you. This is where we need to be every time, with our own level of service. There cannot be an iota of hesitation when it comes to recommendations or referrals from people's shopping experiences with you.

If a salesperson cannot look a customer in the eye and give them the full truth and knowledge that they were open and honest enough to provide the best service possible, then they need to take a long, hard look at themselves.

Imagine seeing a customer who you served at work in the street one day. If the interaction makes you feel awkward enough to cross the street, or if you try to blunder your way through it because you didn't do something you should have or perhaps even lied to your customer, there's an issue with your whole approach.

Sometimes there are personality clashes, of course there are. Not everybody will like you (how dare they?) and that's fine. But as long as you can hold your head up high and acknowledge the fact that you did everything you possibly could, you'll have a clear conscience and can go about your day-to-day life.

A person and the company they represent take a long time to build a good reputation. That can be disregarded immediately if you're not providing impeccable service at all times or if you let your mind wander. Then again, you aren't necessarily providing the best service for the sake of recommendations, you're providing it because that's what the customer deserves. A by-product of that service will then result in referrals and recommendations.

However, both mindsets aren't the correct ones to use when you want to strengthen relationships with customers. Finding that fine line between both emotional states is extremely tricky but can be mastered through mindfulness and increasing your emotional intelligence. Once mastered, you have the ability to navigate through the sales floor in an emotional state that is suitable for its surroundings. You also start to serve customers in the appropriate manner and provide the best possible service.

By doing this, you also become able to work harder and smarter for longer. You'll be more efficient since you're saving energy. Battling with yourself and your emotions is extremely draining and can take up a lot of your emotional capacity. Being emotionally sensitive while guarding your emotional wellbeing and being aware of other people's emotions in the environment you're in is difficult, especially when there are so many you'll come across. However, you must learn to do so, as this is essential for success. Maintaining focus and having the correct mentality and frequency at all times is what allows us to succeed.

I'm a true believer that Earl Nightingale was absolutely correct when he said, "We become what we think about." This could be said for all types of success, whether it be financial, material, or elevating us onto the next chapter of our careers just by changing the emotional state we're in.

Try to remember a time when somebody served you in a store and they were fantastic. The way they helped you and the way they were on hand to answer questions without being pushy. They likely went above and beyond the call of duty to ensure you felt as if your purchase really mattered.

You acknowledged how competent they were, even if it was just to yourself. Maybe you recommended that person to your friends and family. I'm even willing to bet you'd seek them out if you were to go into that store again to make a future purchase. Notice how other members of staff may have looked frazzled in their work, yet this particular salesperson seemed to glide across the showroom with ease. It only made them look even more attractive, and you were drawn into their presence. This is because the more confident you are at completing tasks, the more you will attract customers.

Even when times are hard—pressure from your sales manager, perhaps even an argumentative customer that just won't relent—you must still be that person, regardless of how difficult it may be. You should never be offended or defensive and always deal with what unfolds with grace and dignity, as you'll get more value out of the interaction.

The minute you lose that positive presence, you lose the magnetic energy that helps us draw in and serve customers. To maintain this gravitas and energy on the shop floor, you should come from the correct frequency. There are so many frequencies, but here is a picture from Sir David R. Hawkins, M.D., Ph.D., that describes them best.

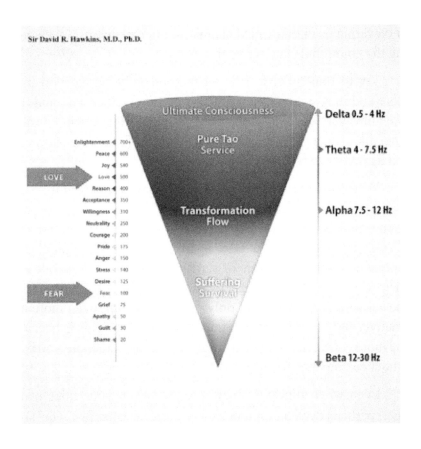

Love, gratitude, and faith are the strongest positive emotions, and when used correctly, they can overcome any feeling of self-doubt.

Nobody wants to be around people with lower frequencies. Napoleon Hill, author of *Think and Grow Rich*, explains how people with high sexual energy acquire and keep the attention of others. Sexual transmutation harnesses that energy by delaying gratification. He mentions how too much of anything will lead even the strongest of men astray, whether that be drink, drugs, or lust. All who have gone on to achieve greatness must first master themselves.

I strongly advise you to read this book cover-to-cover to understand how this and other aspects of his research have benefited the wealthiest people to ever walk the planet. He mentions how using your energy and channeling it into your endeavors will dramatically increase your chances of success. In any scenario, whether it be bad or good, always trying to come from a place of love, gratitude, and faith will open more opportunities for you. This will place you at the correct frequency to attract more success.

People love to be surrounded by positive people, as they're infectious. The mere presence of their energies helps disarm negative emotions or feelings that could potentially be stumbling blocks during the process. Never use negative, sarcastic, or patronizing styles of communication, as this will only lower your vibe.

Ever heard the expression "People buy from happy people"?

Studies show that body language plays a huge part in communication. Studies by Dr. Mehrabian of the University of California show that 70–93% of all communication is nonverbal. Being mindful of your body language at all times is essential to portray a feeling of security, warmth, and confidence to the customer. This research was carried out in the late 1960s and is still applicable today and used by public speaking experts.

I'll go into much more detail in the next chapter about body language, breathing, and voice projection, but our frequency plays a huge part in non-verbal communication too. I think that the foundation of what we consider good is acceptance. Once somebody has found a level of acceptance in whatever scenario they're in, they'll start to let go of their need to control, fight, judge or whatever other saboteurs they start to feel. Instead, they'll look at others' emotions and adapt to the situation. Anything below acceptance will result in resistance within their being. No matter how hard you try to compromise, this energy will then follow through into any interactions they have. In sales, for instance, this will increase resistance as you're trying to force events instead of allowing them to unfold.

This could mean accepting outside scenarios that you have no control over, but it could also mean accepting scenarios that you're also responsible for and doing something about them. Once this level has been achieved, a foundation has been established. Only then can you get the "why" and growth can take place. If this doesn't happen, resentment will only build, which will lead to more stress, frustration, and ultimately bad customer service.

In a state of acceptance, new solutions or methods can be tested until a particular one works. You'll then be able to springboard onto the next task with 100% of the effort and charisma needed to inspire others.

While experiencing these positive emotions and feelings is a great connector, you can't let them take over. Like I'll mention many times in the book, if your emotions spill over, whether they are positive or negative, you'll lose the ability to manage yourself and the sale. Always being in a neutral position, almost as a spectator to the sale, is the only way you'll lower resistance with customers. Unfortunately, salespeople will be seen as biased with their opinions, regardless of whether they're coming from a genuine position or not.

Customers have been programmed to believe they should be wary of salespeople and that care should be taken around them.

This isn't going to change any time soon, so as salespeople, we must change our approach to suit them. Being neutral and not the center of attention like those "alpha" salespeople and allowing customers to make their own mind up in their own time. If you use the skills I'll describe in the coming chapters, you'll also have a certain mystique and endearing quality about your presence.

Having a frequency of love, gratitude, and faith while also being genuine will give you a demeanor of being fun and gentle while still coming across as an authority. You'll have an almost innocent, childlike presence that many people lose when they grow up.

As long as you are your genuine, contained self, that'll shine through, and people will warm to you easier. Nobody is meant to be serious or act like a robot at work all the time. Having a little fun has a positive effect on everybody's well-being. It'll add to the customers' experience too, provided it's warranted.

The thoughts you feed your brain will affect your mood, body language, tonality, and everything else. This is why it's essential that we only feed it positive, reinforcing statements. Positive statements and affirmations can help. Even thinking of a positive experience will help your mood. Have you ever thought back to a holiday so deeply that you could almost feel the same sensation? The power of the mind and visualization are incredible.

You don't just imagine words or sentences either; many other people use different techniques, such as:

- Saying affirmations out loud.

- Tapping the part of your body that the emotional state is anchored into.

- Touching two of your certain fingers or thumbs together to remember the sensation of that feeling or thought.

- Shifting your mindset to a more focused, assertive one.

- Stepping out of other people's stories that are affecting your mentality and behavior.

Whatever you need to do to get back into that emotional state when things aren't going your way is recommended to manage yourself and ultimately the interaction you're in. The more you can manage your thoughts, emotions, and body language, the more influence you'll have in the sale. Resistance will be at an all-time low, and the chance of making a sale dramatically increases.

I like to keep an open and clear mind at all times, which in turn gives me an exterior of calm and composure. Inside, I'm focused and in the zone in my mind. Remember what Charles Xavier explained to Magneto in X-Men? "True focus lies somewhere between rage and serenity." This is what a salesperson's mentality should be.

It helps you to be more receptive. People are more likely to be comfortable with you if you have a cool, relaxed, and soothing aura. Instead of having a million and one ideas, thoughts, or memories racing around your mind, take a second to stop and compose your thoughts. Something that I have accomplished working with Shiraz is that when I rub two fingers together very slowly with enough pressure, I can feel the ridges on each fingertip. I've anchored in a feeling and state that brings me back to a grounded level whenever I am feeling wound up or anxious. Control your breathing; breathe a little deeper. It'll help you regain that state of focus. Untie the knots of nervousness in your stomach and be your true self. No matter what is going on around you, always maintain a clear mind. Your behavior and mannerisms will follow suit.

Too many people in this day and age complain about stress and anxiety. Instead of letting anxiety control you, use it. When used correctly, those traits can be fantastic motivators and should be accepted and embraced rather than avoided. Here is a graph of the Yerkes-Dodson Law from "The Harvard Business Review."

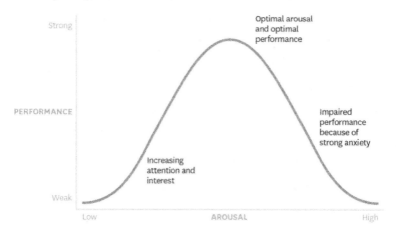

The Yerkes-Dodson Law
How anxiety affects performance.

The chart above shows how stress and anxiety actually help with the level of focus and performance you can achieve when harnessed correctly.

The best salespeople are the ones who can tap into this energy and use it to propel themselves. This is where containing your enthusiasm helps with efficiency. Surrendering yourself to your situation and surroundings helps you deal with the environment you're in. Surrendering doesn't mean waving a white flag and walking away from a situation. It means that you're accepting the situation for what it is without feeling the need to fight it. In the future, you'll be able to conquer and overcome it.

The second you lose control by saying or doing something you know you shouldn't, your anxiety levels can skyrocket, and you can start to lose composure and become stressed. Once you learn to manage this, you can use the adrenaline to slow down what's happening and intercept your surroundings. By intercept, I mean that you become so in tune with your surroundings that you can actually see things happen before they do, and you either prepare yourself for them to take place or step in to intercept.

An example of this is when Ant Middleton, an ex-SAS member and TV host, was trashed in the press because he mentioned how he felt God-like when on a tour in Afghanistan. He was so in the zone that nothing shook his psyche, and he saw events unfold in his mind before they actually happened. I'm not saying sales are the same as going into a hostile war zone, but the principle of channeling your focus into what's happening at present plays a huge part in how efficient you are.

Always try to stay at optimum efficiency, regardless of the scenario. Use breathing techniques and keep a clear but focused mind. You'll help yourself by staying away from self-sabotaging behaviors, negative scenarios, and negative people. You'll learn all of this with experience.

Many salespeople feel the need to be validated by their prospects, which can ruin their sales relationship. The need to feel loved will only lower your standing in the prospects' eyes, and you'll lose your position of authority. Instead, be respected by them. You'll be in a much stronger position, and they'll listen to your words more carefully. Bear in mind, however, you will only be respected by others if you respect yourself. This is where taking care of your own needs comes into play, whether that be through interaction with others or your emotional needs.

Never be in two different mindsets or second-guess yourself when a task needs to be completed. Making decisions and staying true to your goal while having the focus and endurance to maintain the path until completion is a skill that all top salespeople possess. Great salespeople love the grind as well as the good times. They know that by working through the hard times, the fruits of their labor will come. If something happens to make your frequency or energy spike, reassess whether that scenario serves you or not. Be mindful; don't be too harsh in your judgment. Remember that hard times make hard people. Make sure you don't just walk away from a scenario because of a little short-term discomfort.

The Transfer of Energy

Zig Ziglar said sales are the transfer of feelings and beliefs. Therefore, being enthusiastic is important, as customers must believe and feel everything you're explaining for them to buy from you. You must 100% believe in your products and stand behind them every step of the way. If you don't do this, the customer will instantly recognize your hesitation and won't buy. Essentially, people love charismatic, knowledgeable people. Charismatic people make choosing easy for customers and take the pressure away. Once you have them on your side by truly wanting what's best for them, they'll believe anything you say. Not caring what other people think of you, whether they are unruly colleagues or even customers, will give you the confidence to be yourself and inspire others to buy.

Never second-guess what you want to say or stumble with your words. Have a complete, single-minded approach and focus on what is unfolding in front of you rather than what is going on in the background. Only this confidence and charisma will inspire others.

Here's what Simon Sinek said about charisma:

Charisma has nothing to do with energy; it comes from a clarity of WHY. It comes from absolute conviction in an ideal bigger than oneself. Energy, in contrast, comes from a good night's sleep or lots of caffeine. Energy can excite. But only charisma can inspire. Charisma commands loyalty. Energy does not.

Having charisma will inspire the trust and loyalty of our customers. They'll want to keep buying from us, provided we stay in the same state of frequency and energy. We must commit 100% to providing the best solution for any problems that the customer faces; nothing matters more in that moment apart from helping them. Nothing less than 100% commitment and focus going into that task will do. Anything less, and the customer you're interacting with will sniff out uncertainty in an instant.

Here are a few descriptions of salespeople and how they can be categorized straight out of the diary:

Passive - Emotionally dishonest, indirect, inhibited, self-denying, blaming, and apologetic.

"Others needs and rights take priority over my own."

Passive Aggressive - Emotionally dishonest, indirect, and self-denying at first. Self- enhancing at the expense of others later.

"I subtly make clear that my needs and rights prevail."

Aggressive - Inappropriately honest, direct, expressive, attacking, blaming, controlling, and self-enhancing at the expense of others.

"I boldly insist that my needs and rights prevail above all else."

Assertive - Appropriately honest, direct, self-enhancing, expressive, self-confident, and empathic to the emotions of all involved.

"I clearly express that we both have needs and rights."

These are the four behaviors that categorize all sales consultants. Which behavior do you think is best suited for a salesperson? Which behavior do you think you lean towards? Try to be honest with yourself. Maybe it's one specific type. Perhaps it changes from time to time, depending on the circumstances?

I have fluctuated between all four categories in my sales life, but being assertive is by far the best trait to possess. This is because we aren't putting anyone else's needs above our own; instead, we're on an equal footing. That's not to say we don't serve; we absolutely do. We should go above and beyond the level of service required while staying mindful of our own integrity and self-respect. In turn, this will generate rapport between us and the customer. While sometimes having a little aggression can help you stay focused, this must absolutely not spill over into aggressiveness making your customer or client feel uncomfortable.

I consider myself to be a highly sensitive person (HSP), and because of that, I am extremely reactive. I also have a bit of a soft touch in the sense that if somebody gave me a good enough story, I would hand over the last pound in my pocket. That's never a good trait to have in sales! I've had to learn to adjust my behavior in such a way that is not only respectful to the customer but also respectful to the company. I'll go into this in more detail in the following chapters. It's about finding that assertive middle ground that stops us from acting out our natural tendencies.

When I was younger, I would find keeping calm difficult and could quite easily let my emotions control me. However, growing and being able to find that sweet spot in between stress and serenity is where the most efficient work takes place. When I slow down and take the time to concentrate on what's happening in front of me instead of thinking about those what-ifs, I become more effective. People are more inspired by me and want to interact with me. They reveal their true needs. Perhaps it's the other way around, and you're the disagreeable type. Maybe too disagreeable, to the point that you struggle to find common ground with customers and therefore struggle to make sales.

Sometimes we need to learn to reign in our natural reactions in order to achieve our end goal, which is essentially booking business in the correct manner and treating people like people. Remaining neutral is perfect, as it stops us from allowing natural emotional reactions to come to the surface.

Being agreeable is one of the most important traits to have in sales. Even when things are going wrong, customers are losing their minds, and nothing seems to be working the way we want it to, it's imperative to remain agreeable.

Once we're at peace, we slow everything down, including our thoughts. We start to think more clearly and with logic. We start to look after our own emotional well-being. As professional salespeople, we can never react emotionally, as that causes us to lose credibility. We must always be seen as the experts. An expert would never lose control of themselves because they've seen every scenario and know how to navigate them. In this state, we remain in control of the interaction and are the best salespeople we can naturally be. We exude creativity and confidence in a contained manner while generating more and more gravitas into our presence.

Even if a customer is beating us up over an issue or subject, we go back to that frequency of gratitude, a state of calm and neutrality. This stops us from acting out in fear, in-security, or impulse and we start to become mindful. We're setting the benchmark to become pro-active and stay managing the situation.

When serving customers, remember that we are working together to achieve a common goal. You may be gently nudging the customer in the right direction, but you should always let the customer think that they were the ones who were leading the interaction. This process and associated methods are something I'll describe in the coming pages.

Having strong emotional intelligence helps, and by working on ourselves regularly, not engaging in self-sabotage, and being responsible for our own actions, we can not only improve it but also excel at it. Coming from a high-frequency state, being pro-active, and coming from a neutral position, we naturally gravitate towards assisting others in the correct manner.

Because of the frequency with which we're involved, we become the go-to person for help. That's what the best salespeople do, isn't it? We're problem solvers, and we help people with their issues by providing a fantastic solution. Some would say we're actually problem finders, and I'd agree. Salespeople must delve deep into the issues of the customer to find problems without being intrusive or raising sales resistance. We make the process appear effortless. It's our duty and moral obligation to get to the bottom of what's really driving that customer to buy, so we can genuinely provide the best solution possible for their innermost needs.

The customer needs someone on their frequency to help guide them along their journey. Someone who will solve their problems along the way, not cause a fight or a battle. Friction only creates anxiety, resistance, and poor customer service. Instead, make this an act of love and genuine interest, as you're surrendering yourself and delving deep into their "why." You'll challenge their reasoning too, to ensure that their choices are the best possible fit for them. People challenge others out of love and sincerity for their best interests and to help move them forward, so why not do exactly the same with customers in a store?

People you interact with feel your positive energy, whether consciously or subconsciously, and the chances of that interaction remaining positive dramatically increase. This provides better customer service and lets us manage and influence the interaction, providing we articulate our questions correctly.

Sometimes life happens, and you may perhaps forget or lose track of the state you should be in. It could be because of an interaction with somebody, i.e., a customer or a colleague, or because you weren't concentrating enough and lost your train of thought. Whatever happens, it's your job to overcome those challenges and provide the best service.

Remember the name of the game. We're trying to make it as easy as possible for customers to open up and feel comfortable in the environment they're in by lowering that resistance. This is why I don't believe in all these motivational speeches or sales meetings. These are used to psyche people up to the point of becoming emotional and pumped, then they're let loose on the shop floor.

How does the customer feel when some ridiculously over-the-top salesperson tries to interact with them? The customer doesn't care that some motivational music was played or how the team is energized. They just want a salesperson who does their duty and is on their level, helping them potentially make a purchase. Be disciplined enough to keep applying yourself and doing your job to the best of your ability, even on the days when you're tired and feel as if you don't want to continue.

Look at Lou Ferrigno in *Pumping Iron*. He was a fantastic bodybuilder, and his physique was absolutely immense. If we compare him to Arnold Schwarzenegger, we could argue physiques, but let's go deeper into the mindset of the two. Schwarzenegger was, and still is, an absolute winner. Just look at the way he trained. One hundred percent of his absolute focus and energy was going into every single little detail of every single rep. Look how intense he was and how focused he was on channeling all his energy into every minute detail.

Compare this to Ferrigno when he was training with his father. He would be whooping and hollering about how he wanted to beat Schwarzenegger instead of concentrating on the job at hand: using that adrenaline, grounding himself, and channeling it into lifting weights. I think Ferrigno is great, but the fact is that Schwarzenegger knew how to contain his emotional energy, and Ferrigno didn't. That's why Schwarzenegger became the champion.

People used to tell me that I was a great salesman, but I'd always reply that I wasn't a salesman. I was genuinely helping people make an informed choice for themselves, and I enjoyed the process. I was there to assist, not sell. We have to remember that customers enter the store of their own free will and with the intent of shopping. It's a warm market; we aren't cold-calling or knocking on doors. They're here because there is a very high likelihood they want to buy something.

Yes, a small minority of people go into stores to window shop with no intention of buying, but the vast majority do have an intention of buying at some point in the near future. This is why I believe a more relaxed, helpful mindset will work best. This isn't to be confused with a laidback approach, even though in most scenarios that's the impression that should be given.

It's like in *Rocky VI*, when Rocky's son asked him not to go through with the fight. His son said that he didn't look scared. How did Rocky reply?

"Well, you ain't supposed to."

This is exactly the point of being on a shop floor. No matter what pressure is being thrown at us or what scenario is happening, we keep our cool. Fiona Whytehead, who helps people with breathing techniques on stage, quoted it perfectly.

"It's like being a swan swimming graciously on a lake above the water, whilst under the surface, they're paddling furiously."

It's all about the impression we give, and in time, so long as we keep working hard enough and refining our process, that impression or perception will become our reality. But it needs to be in our mind inside and outside of work.

If we truly want to change our psyche and mindset, it needs to be more of a lifestyle choice, rather than just having it in our mind during work hours. If something happened out of our control during work and we responded emotionally because we weren't in the emotional state we should be in, that would affect us for the rest of the day. Of course, there are techniques to bring you back to that correct frequency, but by being aware of your surroundings at all times, you stand a better chance of being at the same level.

It will take so much effort and work to get back into the emotional state that we want to be in. We'll delve deeper into this kind of scenario in the next chapter and discuss how important it is to always have peace of mind. Imagine the emotional rollercoaster that we'd be on. Up and down, up and down. It would be absolutely exhausting. Would you want to do business with somebody like that?

This new-found enthusiasm that we have must be contained. Remember how Schwarzenegger was compared to Ferrigno? Under no circumstances can this emotion leak out or spill over. The second it does, you become giddy, angry, not present, or half-hearted. You lose rapport with the customer, and the chance of making a sale diminishes. It's not impossible, but it's certainly a much harder battle, as the connection between the two of you has been lost. During the entire process, this state of contained enthusiasm must remain constant; under no circumstances should the level of enthusiasm spill over or drop too low. Again, the customer will only be confused by this new persona, and trust will start to diminish. This takes a huge level of focus to attain, but provided that you're immersing yourself in your customers' problems and following important steps, such as getting plenty of rest at night, before long you'll be able to achieve it.

People like constants in their lives. Just look at the sad event of Queen Elizabeth II dying last year; it didn't just hit the world hard because a monarch had died. It was because she was a constant in the vast majority of people's lives. Whenever there was a tragedy, the Queen was there to provide some words of acknowledgement and support. At Christmas, when it was time to rejoice and be happy with our friends and family, the Queen was always there to join us with her own stories of family life while also grounding us with the idea of reflection on what had happened throughout the year. When she passed, all of that went with her. Now it's time for a new monarch; it's time for change. Without getting into a political debate, wherever there is change, there is confusion. Clarity and certainty are key in order to succeed, and keeping our emotional state constant is the only way to do this.

Not only is sales a professional career that can pay a lot of money, but it's a profession that requires us to be at the top of our game. That's what the customer deserves. But we'll also start to attract all manner of other things into our lives because of the energy we're emitting.

Nobody can expect to be a top salesperson when they aren't giving 100% of their focus or having a "That'll do" mindset. There is always somebody working harder to attain that top position, and that's the beauty of sales: competition makes us stronger. It's like the old saying goes, "Steel forges steel."

We must be willing to work hard to be the best we can be. Our enthusiasm and drive must still be as strong as ever, but they must be contained and channeled effectively. Sometimes it's harder and takes longer to get into the right emotional state, depending on how far away from it we are. Let's assume you've been in that focused emotional state all day. It will be easier to put yourself in the same state the next day, assuming nothing major has rocked your being the night before.

Imagine taking a holiday for a week and how your frequency can change. When you come back from holiday and get back into a routine, you notice how hard it is to get back into the swing of things. Everything seems like a chore, and nothing goes as smoothly as it did prior to the break. This is because you aren't on the same frequency that is needed to perform at work. Your metaphorical emotional compass has completely changed direction!

Personally, I try to stay in the same emotional state all holiday, but even I know how unrealistic it is to stay as switched on while on holiday compared to actually being at work. Not to mention, holidays are for connecting and taking time out from the stress of everyday life, so it's not healthy. The more you've gone off the frequency, the more you've lost your head, and the harder it is to get back on that level. This is why I never recommend straying too far from the frequency you're on and living a more consistent life.

When I was younger, I would have a week off, then come back to work and "forget" how to sell. I'd use a strong frequency that was self-serving, and nothing would work. That's what spending a fortnight in Ibiza will do to you! As soon as I toned down my frequency to help others, the orders came flooding in.

If you're in any doubt when you're struggling to close deals, build rapport with customers. If you feel like you've lost your mojo, start to serve people unconditionally, with faith, and without an agenda. This will get the ball rolling. That leads to confidence and assertiveness. Be so in the zone that nothing else exists apart from you and your customer.

Setting the Stage - Part 2 (Added Bonus)

Notice how when you are standing rigidly, with your shoulders raised and chest puffed out, you're emitting a strong vibe that could actually be quite off-putting to the customer. Try it now, put the book down, and give your best power pose. Perhaps your hands are on your hips, portraying that image of authority and attitude. Would you be completely comfortable being served by somebody in that manner, or would it be a little intimidating?

It's our job to lure the customer into our presence and make them feel relaxed during their experience. I'm going to explain exactly how to do that.

When you're working in your store or in any sales career, you're automatically seen as the authority figure. Couple this with the professional apparel you're wearing, and you've got it tied down to a tee. This means that you don't try too hard to gain the trust of the customer; if anything, when you try too hard, it will raise the customer's sales resistance, making it even harder for you to break through. Using these "power stances" may make you feel assertive and in charge, but is it what the customer needs? Or is it just what you need to make yourself feel that way?

Perhaps you're working under pressure and feel the need to show how important you are. Maybe you're working with colleagues and trying to fight your way up the food chain, or maybe you're feeling a little down and need to put on this act of confidence.

In reality, this is all bravado and not an act of confidence at all. Having self-confidence means being comfortable with yourself, no matter what the surroundings are, and allowing yourself to actually be yourself, regardless of the situation. Of course, sometimes you fake it 'til you make it, but when you're truly confident in yourself, customers will notice this and open up to you more easily. They'll trust you. In order to do this, you must let go of your insecurities, fear of judgment, and anything else that may be holding you back. Allow yourself to show the customer your vulnerable side. Sometimes I still tense my jaw in order to feel confident enough to put myself in positions that aren't in my comfort zone, but then I try my best to counteract this behavior by being mindful.

Feel free to use power poses to set yourself up for the day, in the privacy of your own room, or even on the way to work. Feeling powerful can be part of getting your mind and body in a confident mode for meetings and interactions. That is what they are useful for—to help you feel the part deep inside.

Notice how when you're feeling insecure, your body may start expressing that by tightening up. Some people mention how their solar plexus starts to tighten or their hands start to become more rigid. Personally, when I'm feeling anxious, my jaw naturally goes extremely tight, and I start to stand more rigidly.

When you let the adrenaline get the better of you, your behavior changes. Your body will then reflect that. You start to lose self-control and therefore, have less ability to influence. A master salesperson will manage their entire being, and communication, to ensure that the customer has the best experience. If there was ever a chance they were going to buy, they would because of that.

Stand up and raise your shoulders all the way up to your neck, so it almost looks as if you don't have one. Then, after a few seconds of really raising your shoulders as far as they'll go, I want you to drop them to their natural position. Notice how good that feels? This is where your shoulders need to be at all times. Whenever you're presenting, conversing, or interacting with customers, or any other people for that matter, never let your shoulders rise above this level.

When you do raise them, you're acting in a defensive manner. It's an instant defense mechanism that we all have once we have a little confrontation or something happens that we don't particularly like. This could be with a colleague, a customer, or anyone. By keeping your shoulders at a natural level, you're emitting a vibe that whatever is unfolding in front of you isn't phasing you.

Next, I want you to stand up as you would when serving a customer, shoulders in natural position, and then put a slight bend in your knees. Don't let yourself go to jelly and fall to the floor; there should be no resistance in the way that you're standing. Your body will naturally do its job and hold you upright. Can you feel how much more relaxed you are? Do you notice how much better you feel? You've most likely got much less on your mind now since you're in a more casual state.

You're still the professional salesperson that customers need, but you're not the typical professional salesperson they see in every other store. You're now the warm, casual, professional salesperson who genuinely chooses to help the customer find the product or service they need. Not the typical one that has to put on a big show and bravado of how they feel they've got to do it. See the difference? Who would you rather be served by?

Notice how I mentioned lowering the resistance in your body? All the resistance that you have will naturally raise a customer's sales resistance. You may feel that it makes you more important, but it doesn't help lower sales resistance from a customer and is actually a show of insecurity.

Fiona Whytehead of *Locus Coaching* has some really useful exercises. They ensure that your body language is giving the right signals to your audience and that you are feeling relaxed and confident in your own skin. If you feel it, it will come across to your clients as such.

For example, the way I learned how to stop my jaw from clenching is by using my second and third fingers and massaging gently behind my ear lobes. In this exercise, you allow your mouth to open slightly and your tongue to drop down onto the floor of your mouth. You should also feel your neck relaxing and your throat opening up as well. The way you speak plays a huge part in the way you come across too. Remember that sales are the transfer of energy, and your voice plays a crucial part in that. Projecting your voice is not about shouting but about speaking on the out breath through an open throat.

As Fiona Whytehead, a speaking and presence skills expert and confidence expert, says:

"Full breathing is crucial to being heard, trusted, and liked when you are speaking or selling. No question."

Creating a full, rounded voice and being able to use your nervous energy as a way to light you up rather than bring you down in terms of speaking in public.

We need to take in more breath to thrive than just to survive.

You can survive by breathing in small, shallow breaths, a habit the majority of us take up as we grow up, and the things people say or our experiences put us on our guard.

However, shallow breathing, where the breath only fills the top of our lungs and doesn't get beyond the very upper part of our chest, will create a thin-sounding voice, noticeable fear, or a lack of energy in how we are presenting. Ultimately, you will not make the positive connection that you are seeking with your audience.

As the renowned voice teacher Patsy Rodenburg says in her book, *Presence*, "All human energy is breath. The body houses you, and breath powers you. It's the first act you perform, and it is the last. Breath powers your body, your voice, your mind, your heart, and your spirit."

Looking at how babies breathe, with their tummies going up and down, up and down, we can see how we were born to breathe. Bring to mind how well they utilize their voice to get attention.

A baby's cry comes from the pit of their stomach. They breathe in fully, filling their lungs, and then let go.

Full breathing means fully engaging your diaphragm muscle, a dome-shaped muscle that sits below your heart and your lungs. It acts like a pair of bellows to suck the air in when you breathe and exhale it out. The inward and outward movements in your body when you breathe in and out should be in your stomach. Your upper chest and shoulders should remain still.

The issue for us is that when we get nervous, we naturally tend to tense up in our upper chest and tighten our shoulders. This impedes full breathing action. Getting nervous before speaking in public is totally natural and common. Even the most confident of us still get nervous when we speak in public; after all, no one can be completely sure of what will happen when we do.

Nervousness, or the adrenaline that we create when we are nervous, can also be a good thing. It can be a fun feeling (excitement) or an unpleasant one (fear). To speak well, convincingly, and be trusted by your audience, you need to get this totally naturally occurring feeling. Use it to your advantage to light up rather than close down. Resist the urge to tense up and engage with your breath; open up in your rib cage and support your voice from your stomach.

Learn to breathe as we were born to breathe, and your words will have the meaning and momentum that you desire each time you speak. Being on a shop floor, depending on the kind you work on, can be extremely aggressive. There's a natural tendency to go into our shell. I certainly felt that, and sometimes I still do. I clam up and tighten up instead of relaxing and breathing fully from the diaphragm.

When I remembered that this was essential to creating a presence of trust and confidence, people were drawn to me more and opened up about their true needs. Yes, this shows a little vulnerability because you've put yourself truly out there, but this is the only way that you'll inspire people enough for you to lead them. Rise above the politics, ignore the aggression, and concentrate on being the best version of yourself. My energy and spirituality coach, Shiraz Baboo, mentions how, in order to truly fall in love, you must be willing to have your heart broken. This analogy is perfectly appropriate for sales too. It's this level of unconditional giving and showing short-term vulnerability that will elevate your capacity.

For more information on Shiraz and his work, check out his website, www.energeticmagic.com.

While breathing from the diaphragm and keeping your enthusiasm contained are essential to influence, salespeople should always be at the same frequency as the customer. Imagine you're serving a customer who is metaphorically "simmering away" at 200 degrees Fahrenheit. You must then alter your approach to simmering at the same level of 200 degrees.

As the sale progresses, if the customer changes their frequency, a professional salesperson has the emotional intelligence to move along with them as they alter their temperature while keeping their enthusiasm simmering away. This takes a lot of emotional intelligence and an element of drama, but over time and with experience, you'll learn this if you're mindful of your behavior.

Fiona reminds us to think back to when you yawned and opened both your nasal and throat airways. Try to yawn now to feel the sensation again. Whenever presenting or speaking, these passages must be open, so what you're saying comes out clear, concise, and full of confidence. This also allows your voice to resonate, so that it sounds full, rich, and warm. Your words will also come across in a manner that everybody will be able to hear and take note of. You'll speak more assertively, and that energy will transfer to the recipient. Your presence will have more gravitas. People's ears will start to prick up as you know what you're talking about, inspiring more confidence.

Where you place your hands is also essential to communication. They certainly can't be in your pockets, as this will portray an image of disinterest in what's going on around you. They can't be behind your back either. This also gives the impression that you're trying to be an authority figure and will raise resistance in yourself and the customer. It's an "I'm here and you're there" mentality instead of a "We're in this together" approach.

When you're concentrating on your knees being slightly bent, keeping both your airways open, and articulating correctly, there isn't much room to be unsure where to put your hands. Your hands will naturally fall into a position that's comfortable and will suit the demeanor and frequency that you're sending out.

Only when you aren't concentrating on these points will your hands fall into unnatural positions, and you'll start to feel socially awkward. Whenever you're concentrating on your body language and behavior, everything else falls into place because of the focus you're giving them.

Gesticulating is a fantastic way of expressing your point and communicating clearly. Like any communication style, it must be carried out in a controlled and contained manner. Using hands to make gestures will only add to your profile, and people will be drawn to your presence and gravitas.

These behaviors may seem strange at first but try them out and keep using them. You'll feel so much better within yourself, be less stressed, and provide fantastic service.

Chapter 2

The night before the next day at work is one of the most important factors in succeeding in sales. If we're prepared properly, we can excel. If not, we'll fall by the wayside.

Like Benjamin Franklin said, "By failing to prepare, you are preparing to fail."

In order to have an efficient and productive day at work, you need to pay attention to the finer details. Energy flows where you let it, whether that be into positive situations or negative ones. That's why making sure we manage our energy through emotional awareness helps us give our best and live up to our true potential.

My life wasn't all about staying focused and harnessing my energy, though. For many years, my night before consisted of partying, drinking, and indulging in inappropriate behavior. Very often, I would drive to cities across the UK to see what the night would bring, with absolutely no plan of where my friends and I would go or where we would stay. More often than not, I'd end up at a trashy house party or even crashing in the back of the car in a high-rise car park after stumbling across a rave that went on into the next day. I'd never had the freedom to be my own person, so when I was on a night out or a weekend away, I really went to town.

When I had a bad day at work, I wouldn't go home and reflect on why I was having a bad day. I never ran through the scenario that triggered me. I never asked myself the important questions.

"What could have been done or said differently?"

"Who or what was at fault?"

"How am I at fault, and what could I do better in the future?"

I had zero mindfulness, faith, patience, or persistence and wasn't responsible for my own actions. I would fly off the handle, arguing and shouting, making myself look like a fool in the very early days. Then I'd go out partying to forget my problems. As we all know, this behavior stems from avoiding issues and isn't the correct way to deal with them. Taking them head-on is the only way to confront and conquer your demons, no matter how difficult they may be.

I'd hang around with people who weren't necessarily good for my personal growth or career, but we had a similar mind when it came to that culture. That's not to say I blame anybody else for what I did; I don't. My actions were my own, and I made a conscious decision. I did what I wanted to do at that particular moment, and to be completely honest with you, I enjoyed much of what I did. Even though, towards the end of my mid-twenties, I knew that if I was going to succeed, I had to take life more seriously.

This is why I believe work is so important in our lives. Whether it's an entrepreneurial business that we're running or sweeping the streets for the local authority, work gives us discipline and a reason to get up in the morning. It gives us structure and routine, provides us with mental stimulation, and helps us socially by interacting with different people. Sales even more so.

Not to mention it provides us with money, which in turn gives us the life we want.

While I have always worked since a young age–about seven–I never really had a true direction in my life. Even though I have always tried my hardest and ultimately been fantastic at what I do, there is no real meaning or end goal in sight. There was a point, however, when an opportunity came up in one of the stores I was working in to really put my stamp on the world. It was like having an epiphany.

Within a few weeks of my new attitude, I found a new depth to my abilities. I was able to express myself a little bit more, and creativity started to spill out of me. I would tell others that I wouldn't be going out partying because I had work commitments, and instead, I would stay in, recharging my batteries for the next day. This protected my emotional well-being. There was absolutely no way I could go out drinking and partying, lose my mind, and then just walk into a high-pressure sales world the next day. Not if I wanted to perform to the standard I was capable of. My priorities had changed.

So many people have said that in the past, "I sell more when I'm hungover; I just go on autopilot," or other associated excuses. I even used to think that, and what a load of rubbish it is. Maybe we did sell some products when we were still feeling the effects of the alcohol the night before, but it wasn't out of skill or competence. It was lucky!

And regardless, did the customer have a fantastic experience? When there're being served by a salesperson who's still half-baked, with beer breath, and not really interested because they're miles away living in cloud cuckoo land. Absolutely not! I would implore every salesperson who is reading this to not drink the night before work. You'll be fresher, sharper, be able to manage your thoughts and emotions, and provide a fantastic service. Leave the drinking until you're off the next day, though you shouldn't drink at all, it'll pay dividends, I promise.

Maybe ask yourself why you're drinking and partaking in self-sabotaging behaviors. Is there an issue that needs to be addressed or that you're avoiding? Is it escapism? If that's the case, I insist that you deal with those issues and traumas, no matter how hard they may be. It's difficult to deal with past issues, but the payoff in the long term far outweighs the short-term pain. This is such a hard task, as very often you must look at yourself and admit the mistakes that you've made along the way, but in any walk of life, it's necessary to grow.

Having hard but reasonable conversations with your managers, colleagues, friends, and families may upset them or even rock the boat, but you'll be better off having them. Plus, you'll learn to live and excel with the outcome. People grow in different directions, and sometimes boundaries need to be created. If you've outgrown someone or a situation, address it and see if you can move things forward. If not, have a look at the relationship and see if you should cut it off.

Sabotaging behavior doesn't just mean drinking, drugs, or eating disorders. It could be over-exercising and other behaviors that may seem good on the surface but can have a negative effect in the long term. Good things can become harmful when they're used to an extreme instead of dealing with suppressed emotions. By dealing with emotions, we become the people we're supposed to be. Since becoming sober, I've walked away from relationships that don't serve me and have since started mixing with people who are ambitious, intelligent, and want to succeed.

Not taking action out of fear is the worst decision you can ever make. You have one chance on this planet, and there are no second chances. How do you want to reflect on your life when you're on your deathbed? Will you reflect on it with regret? Or will you look back with a little smile on your face knowing that you went out, gave it your all, and achieved your goals, or at the very least, gave them a shot?

Jim Rohn famously said, "We are the average of the five people we spend the most time with," and I can categorically say this is true. If you want to change your circumstances, you need to look at your circle of peers and see if they are where you would like to be in 5 years. This goes for both friends and family. If you join a circle where there are five alcoholics, you'll be the sixth. If you're with five millionaires, the chances are you'll be the sixth. If somebody is not in your alignment or, even worse, is tearing you away from your alignment for their own gain or insecurity, they should be eliminated from your life.

Negative people take up so much emotional energy. They have the capacity to suck you dry, leave you holding the baby like it was nobody's business, and spin the events on you, but only if you let them. I talk about coming from a place of faith, love, and open heartedness, but negative people have a lesser capacity for this. However, it's not your job to change their point of view. They're on their path in life, and if they want to change their direction, they're going to have to change it themselves. If they don't, that's their choice.

We all know about our financial bank accounts. But what about our emotional accounts? Which one do you think is more important? Without a shadow of a doubt, our emotional account takes precedence over our financial account. Why? Because without our emotional and spiritual energy to give us the drive to get up every morning and be productive, nothing would happen, and we would start to regress.

Look at past lottery winners and how they won an absolute fortune that changed their lives, only to lose it all a few years later. This is because they entered into behaviors that were not aligned with being successful, or at a minimum, being reasonable and responsible. They were stuck at that poor frequency, and their actions led to their bankruptcy.

There are so many stories about how millionaires, even billionaires, became self-made and lost it all, only to come back and make it again, and more! These are the mindsets of winners. They're positive, optimistic, and open to learning. They know that by looking after themselves emotionally and spiritually, they will attract opportunities and take advantage of them when they show up.

We wake up and have our emotional battery at 100%; we can't charge any more. The second we let negative people into our psyche, they start to drain that battery. Let's say we have an argument with a spouse first thing in the morning; that could take 10% of our battery, and then we enter into an argument because of road rage on the way into work. That's another 10% gone. All of a sudden, we're down to 80%, and that's provided we're fresh from the night before.

How are you supposed to compete at a high level in the sales world on anything less than 100%? You'll never achieve your true potential if you don't dedicate yourself and prioritize what's really important to you. Maybe you don't have the guts to finish a relationship because of what other people think or because you're scared of what will happen if you do. Perhaps it's finally making a decision and starting on something that you've wanted to do for years, but you come up with excuses about how you're "too busy." Or if it wasn't because of "X," I'd be doing "Y." This paralysis will only fester and stop you from living your best life.

Learn to loosen your control and let things unfold naturally; they may not work out the way you had hoped, but you won't have regrets and will have learned lots along the way.

I also have an issue with manufactured energy. I believe that being self-motivated and disciplined enough to dig deep and find motivation is the best method for success, rather than relying on a product. We've touched on the facts and benefits of having a clean life, staying away from drinking and drugs, etc. But what about other stimulants? Caffeine is a drug, and although it may not be as bad as the ones that are exported from Columbia, it's a stimulant nonetheless.

I'm not telling you to quit your morning coffee, but I am asking you to at least consider it, especially if you're of a sensitive nature. Living a clean life away from stimulants and depressants will help you deal with and regulate your emotions better. You shouldn't rely on coffee, Red Bull, or any other energy drink to give you that edge. Find that edge by working harder and getting into that motivated state on your own merit; it'll feel better, and you'll have more satisfaction from it. We then think more clearly, are our true selves, and have a much better chance of creating a genuine connection with customers.

Since I'm a highly sensitive person, the effects of caffeine blow my mind. There was absolutely no way I could provide a fantastic mindful service when my thoughts were all over the place. They needed to be managed, focused, and channeled into articulated words that were communicated clearly to the customer. Any activity that has the slightest chance of damaging that needs to be removed.

Your relationship with yourself is more important than any other relationship. I once attended an awards event where the keynote speaker was a man called Lord Rumi Verjee, and he explained this perfectly. Lord Rumi was an immigrant from East Africa who came to the UK as a child. Lord Rumi had nothing but amazing passion and a huge will to win. At the age of just 28, he spent the last of his money to buy a ticket to the States to meet with the unsuspecting man who owned Domino's Pizza. Lord Rumi explained how he had absolutely no experience in the pizza business and no clue how to run a store, but he knew he would make it work. The American business owner was so impressed with his passion, enthusiasm, and faith that he gave him a shot and let Lord Rumi take the franchise back home. Within months, he had expanded up and down the country and finally sold his shares for well into the tens of millions.

He was asked how he got to where he was and how he became so successful. He said, "First, you must look after yourself. Then you must look after your family, then your community, and then, if possible, the world."

Looking after yourself first gives you a better platform to provide a brighter future for your family. If you're not fit mentally, physically, emotionally, or spiritually, it is nearly impossible to provide that future.

Not many people have the awareness or confidence to do what is right for them. They do what's easy, they do what they've always done, or they do what their so-called friends do out of fear of being disliked and judged. Many people do what their parents want because that's what their parents told them. Then, years down the line, they're deeply unhappy because of the choices they've made and are bitter pessimists towards the world. All because they took the easy route rather than the one that they really wanted to take but didn't because it was too hard to stand alone and away from the crowd.

Nobody ever got anywhere in life strictly by being liked. The most successful people in the world, whether they were business-people, athletes, or actors, were absolutely ruthless in their approach and worked their butts off. When we aren't mindful, we forget that looking after our own wellbeing is important not just to us but to the people around us too. Taking the time to do what's right for us personally not only helps us disconnect, but it also provides us with a new lease on life and an opportunity to go again with increased vigor.

Delaying gratification plays a huge part in this, but it's not just declining to go out for drinks that makes the difference. It's in the little things, like making sure your car is filled with gas when it flashes empty. Yes, this may seem obvious, but how many times have you thought, "It'll be okay; it'll get me to work tomorrow"? But this isn't the attitude of a winner. Winners plan meticulously and leave nothing to chance. Imagine waking up to-morrow and forgetting that your car needs gas. That stress you'd feel wondering if you were going to make it to work or not. You've just lost another 2%!

These little tasks create momentum, and once enough mo-mentum has been generated, we start to become confident and assertive. I'd ensure I was in bed at a reasonable hour to give me sufficient sleep, which I recommend everybody should do. Per-sonally, I cannot function properly on less than seven hours of sleep a night, preferably eight. But you must decide how many hours you need; everybody is different. However, once you de-cide, you must stick to it.

Before bed, I would ensure my work uniform was ready for the next day, so there'd be no stumbling around in the morning wondering where my tie was or if my shoes were polished. Everything was laid out the night before in preparation. I'd then envision myself on the shop floor actually wearing the outfit that I had picked. I would see myself serving customers, writing up orders, and being successful in that exact outfit. That was the state of focus I was in at all times; it didn't matter that I was at home. The point of this was that the whole cycle was a process, and every moment rolled into one, whether it be hours through the working day or even when going to sleep. It wasn't just for the job; it was a lifestyle choice.

It's funny because Dorian Yates mentioned on a podcast how he practiced the exact same method of visualizing. For example, he would picture what he would wear to the gym the night before. He then went on to become Mr. Olympia. It's awesome to think that greats like him were practicing the exact same habit. What we wear is so important in sales, as first impressions absolutely do count.

Yes, we've been told not to judge a book by its cover, but the fact is, we're all humans, and we do judge. If somebody is scruffy-looking and smells like they haven't had a shower for the past few days, we will not want to interact with them, let alone do business with them. That's a fact. A salesperson should always look their absolute best, and below is a brief description of what men and women should wear:

Men - A quality plain shirt with pants accompanied by a sleek professional tie. Perhaps a suit if you feel comfortable. I never wore a suit, as I never felt myself wearing one.

Women - A classy business suit or very professional dress. Nothing provocative.

There's a saying that goes something like, "You can tell a lot about a person by their shoes." I would always spend the bulk of my clothing budget on shoes, as they can make or break a personal style. Any good-quality brand will suffice, and make sure they're regularly polished. Nothing is more off-putting than somebody coming across as an authority figure with scuffed shoes.

You don't go to a designer store or spend thousands of dollars, but certainly a budget shirt and pants won't do. You can identify cheap clothes a mile away, and in a face-to-face retail environment, we need to make the best impression we possibly can. If you're wearing a tie, make sure your top button is fastened and the tie is worn correctly! There is nothing worse than that casual sleazy salesman. Wear your tie properly, or don't wear it at all. Making the investment and taking the time to choose good quality clothing will pay off tenfold.

I appreciate that we're in the 21st century, but I'm also a big believer in traditional values when it comes to sales. This is why I'm dead set against tattoos being shown on a shop floor. I actually love tattoos and have many, but in a professional setting, unless you're a Harley-Davidson salesman, I don't believe there is room for them. I've actually chosen to have a tattoo removed from my hand because it wasn't professional and gave the wrong impression. Keeping them covered up looks more professional and gives the impression to all customers that you're respectable and trustworthy. You're more than likely a trustworthy person with the tattoo, but it's the customer who makes that decision, so their perception matters most. If there is any room for a potential sale to walk, it's got to go.

The same goes with beards. Maybe a goatee or a well-kept trimmed moustache could be ok but an all-out beard? This is never a good look on a shop floor and in an ideal world a salesperson should be clean shaven at all times. As we've discussed, the energy sex brings can help us make more sales when channeled correctly. However, a woman or man should never be dressed provocatively, it shows a lack of self-respect and completely trashes their image.

Never flirt with a customer, even if there are sparks flying and the level of rapport is really deep. It's completely inappropriate and will ruin your frequency. The would be a perfect example of letting your contained enthusiasm spill over because you weren't managing your emotions correctly. Always remember that you're there to serve in a professional setting. We must provide an image of professional leadership, respect, and authority. Somebody who the potential customers can look up to and confide in. We'll also feel great and confident within ourselves, so it's a win-win.

I'd also think of the most important tasks that I had to complete and mentally check them off in my brain. I'd visualize myself working on the tasks and going through the options that were needed to create a positive outcome. This meant they were engrained in my subconscious, so when they actually happened, it felt almost like a memory, so the conversation flowed more seamlessly. Then, when the morning came, I was full of energy to take on the challenge rather than dreading waiting to see what happened. By being proactive in my approach and taking the challenge head-on, I set my energy at a much higher frequency level and spurred myself on to succeed in all tasks that I undertook. The same still applies today.

Obviously, sometimes things happened that were unforeseen, but I found that exciting too! Going to work prepared to expect the unexpected is an awesome mentality to have. You never know what's going to happen tomorrow, but you accept that, and then you're prepared for whatever is thrown at you and ready to take on the challenge. When unexpected situations arise, you keep your cool and emotions in check through mindfulness and either maneuver around them or deal with them accordingly. You then start to become accountable and look at situations in a mature manner, without becoming a victim of circumstance.

It's similar to when a little baby tortoise hatches on a beach and has to get to the sea. It knows what it must do, but in order for it to get there, that little creature has got to open itself up to the world, leave its comfort zone, and take a chance. I'd visualize my success for the next day every night, and that visualization helped me get into the right frequency to follow through.

There was a study with three groups of basketball players a few years ago. The three groups all threw free throws, and the number of shots they scored was recorded. One group then spent a month practicing free throws, one group sat in a classroom, visualizing and scoring free throws, while the other group sat in a classroom and did nothing.

After the month was over, each group was tested again, and their shot rate was counted. The ones who sat in a classroom doing nothing didn't increase their shot rate. The ones who had been physically practicing free throws increased their rate by 27%, and the ones who had only been visualizing scoring free throws increased their rate by 26%! This is the power of the mind.

Making ourselves accountable by dealing with issues and becoming responsible for our actions helps us become confident and competent. Never try to put your head in the sand when issues arise; they'll only grow and become worse. This will then have a negative effect on your well-being and cause more stress. Jeff Bezos once said, "Stress comes from not dealing with your problems."

So set your alarm for the following day. Make sure you're giving yourself enough time to get up and complete your morning ritual while also ensuring you've had enough sleep.

Very often I used to, and still do, go over conversations in my mind that have happened during the day, little glances that happened between people, and subtle cues that I may not have picked up during the day when interacting with people. By doing this, I pieced together scenarios and tried to get what kind of people I was conversing with, whether they be customers or more in particular, colleagues. I'd run through scenarios to try and get the context of what had been said and whether they were a person I could trust or not. This sounds extremely intense, and I suppose it is, but to be number 1, you should be two steps ahead of everybody else, especially in sales. As my emotional intelligence increased, I became more aware and was able to suit my behavior towards others in acceptance of who they were.

Since I've gotten older, I've also taken note of what I dream and how my dreams can be interpreted. I'm a huge believer that dreaming taps into our subconscious and that allowing our dreams to flow plays a huge part in our self-growth. If something is happening in your reality, whether you're aware of it or not, your dreams will help determine what action you should take. Dreaming helps us deal with underlying issues we may have in our "woke world," and I advise you to allow your dreams to play out and trust your intuition.

Since taking note of my dreams, I have become much more self-aware and feel connected to my true self. So many times, I dreamt of an obscure vision, only for it to unfold and turn out to be true weeks or months down the line. Dreaming would have played a huge part in my sales career too, but in all honesty, I didn't pay it much attention. Sure, my presence and mindset would have changed, but I didn't really take note of the who, what, and why; I just kind of went about my day. If I had been as aware of my dreams back then as I am now, I'm fairly certain I would have been much more successful in my career. Please use this as an opportunity to tap into your subconscious, as I believe it will help you with your work and make you a better person.

Here's an example of a dream I had very recently. Bear with me because it's quite intense. I came to a crossroads in my business and had to make a choice. I weighed up all the options and chose to go down a path, even though I knew it didn't align with me spiritually and wasn't the next logical step in the process. That night I had the most vivid dream that I bought a shotgun, went into a post office with my friends, and robbed it at gunpoint. I dreamt how I was on the run, scared, and eventually the police caught up with me.

Crazy right?

I woke up the next day in shock, as it was one of those dreams that felt like it could have happened. I googled the meaning later that day, and many people interpreted the dream to mean that they're taking short cuts in life to get where they want to go and that they may rethink their decisions in order to take the right path to the future they want.

This could be a complete coincidence, but the meaning was spot on. I was taking a shortcut to the life I wanted and overlooking the correct procedure in order to lay the foundation for the rest of the process. I then altered my approach to the more aligned, long-term method and instantly felt more at ease. I knew the groundwork I was putting in was correct.

This is very similar to serving customers, which is why I believe I did extremely well. Nothing was ever out of sync with the process of what needed to happen. I would never rush a customer into making a decision; I would never show options unless they were ready to see them; and I would never bring up solutions or facts unless the timing was right. People are sensitive creatures and appreciate it when things unfold smoothly in a seamless order. It makes the decision-making process easy.

This is difficult, especially when there is sales pressure. However, this is the only way you'll be the top salesperson while keeping, building, and strengthening those relationships. Empathy and high emotional intelligence are essential for this, as the process must always suit the customer and their needs. Sure, you know what's got to be asked in order to get the information you need to complete the sale, but extracting that information must unfold naturally in the customer's timing. You must make sure they feel comfortable enough to discuss and answer questions. Whenever you try to force something, sales resistance rises, and the chances of the sale walking away increase.

Trial and error are a huge part of this, as you'll never always get it right. Having the wisdom, grace, and accountability to admit that will help you change for the better. I was always excited about going to bed since I knew tomorrow would be another day at work, and I still feel that way today. What will happen? What will I learn? How will I overcome the challenge? Every single day is a blessing, and having the mindset and energy that you can't wait to get up the next day is phenomenal.

Always remember that if you've had a bad day, the second you go to sleep, you're hitting the reset button, and tomorrow will be completely different.

Chapter 3

Waking Up & Getting into Work

On hearing the alarm, when in the right energy, you'll be ready to spring out of bed. You'll feel excited to head to work and see what challenges the day brings. This mood is infectious, but it must be harnessed and contained. Never let this energy spill over, or you'll definitely run the risk of losing composure for the day ahead. You're up right away, and the first job of the day is to make your bed. Have you seen the video of Admiral William H. McRaven addressing the University of Texas? He gives a fantastic presentation on how such a mundane task can give you a sense of accomplishment. It gives you encouragement that leads you to do another and another. The same principle is applied here.

Confidence isn't just about completing big tasks. Confidence comes from doing what you should be doing regularly. Ed Mylett articulates it perfectly by saying it comes from keeping promises to yourself. By keeping promises to yourself, we achieve little victories that then give us momentum and motivation to do the next task. As momentum builds, confidence levels start to increase, as do our capabilities. It's here, however, that we must keep our feet on the ground. Otherwise, we run the risk of becoming arrogant, which is never a good look. Using our affirmation helps keep this in check, as well as helping us find our momentum.

Then I'd get a cold shower to clean and invigorate my senses, and then I'd be ready for the day. Sometimes in the past, I've gotten up too late and didn't take a shower, and it had an effect on my mentality all day long. Having habits that we practice daily, no matter how small, sets us up for success. The human body and mind need routine to eliminate stress.

Imagine how cranky a child gets when he or she isn't in a routine. Perhaps they go to bed a little later than usual. Perhaps they perform an activity that's a little out of sync with their normal day. This normally (depending on the temperament of the child) ends up in tears or, at a minimum, making the child extremely sleepy. But when in a routine, the child is happy and carefree because they have structure in their lives. Just because we're adults, this doesn't change.

Once you're clean and ready, put on the exact outfit that you visualized the night before. Notice how it doesn't even feel like you're putting it on; it's almost like a second skin. After splashing on some cologne and drinking a pint of water, I was on my way out the door with the intent of having a fantastic day and serving customers to the best of my ability.

I never used to eat breakfast, but my advice is that if you do, eat something healthy and light. The last thing you need inside of you is something heavy or greasy that could hinder your mindset and energy levels.

The reason I never ate breakfast was because I enjoyed the discipline of fasting. Knowing that I was hungry but delaying the gratification of giving in and eating kept me focused, and I became mentally stronger. I would do this throughout the day before making the choice to eat lunch. Not to mention, if there were customers to be served, there was no way I would ever leave them just for the sake of a sandwich, wherever I worked. Wherever there was money to be made, the money came first, every time. I always found that I would eat as a coping mechanism out of stress, and I found that if I broke through that barrier of giving in to the temptation, I was stronger and more confident for it.

Maybe you've got a behavioral pattern when you're under stress? Like going to the toilet, checking your phone, making drinks, going for a cigarette, or gossiping. Once you eliminate these impulses from your behavior, you'll be much more confident, efficient, and productive.

On the way to work in my car, I'd be clearing my mind for the day ahead. I'd get in at the right frequency that was needed to be successful at work and make those critical connections. I would have the stereo off, as for me, it was and still is way too much of a distraction. Music plays a huge factor in determining the frequency you're at; that's why we listen to it. The frequencies at a rave compared to those at a classical theater are completely polarized. People gravitate towards their chosen frequencies due to their specific tastes and energy levels. Listening to 90's rave on the morning commute? Sure, it might be nice to reminisce about the good old days, but it's not exactly going to put you in the right kind of mood to work productively.

The frequency I was in had to be rock tight from the moment I closed my eyes to the second I opened them. Looking back, I used to get quite annoyed about how I would be at a different frequency when I woke up, but it was necessary. As I've mentioned before, dreaming helps sort out the subconscious issues we're having.

Imagine playing Adele on the way to work and crying, or rocking out to AC/DC. That emotional frequency is so far off from where you need to be entering work and being at your potential to sell right off the bat. It would take an age to get back down to the level you need to be to function correctly. Try thinking of an old radio or TV where you would spend hours trying to dial into that perfect frequency to get the right channel. Think back to how temperamental it was and how delicate it needed to be in order for it to work correctly. The same applies here!

Think of how many opportunities would be missed just because you lost your concentration. It's really not worth it. The same goes with listening to the news, as there is so much negativity around these days. Feeding that to your brain will have a detrimental effect. Always try to stay away from negative stories that will affect your mood; if you don't, you're subconsciously sabotaging your chances of success. Brian Tracy mentions turning your car into a university on wheels by listening to podcasts, CDs, or cassettes. Fair play to Brian for having that mentality, but for me, I like to be in the zone, ready to take on the day ahead.

Instead, I would imagine myself being the top salesperson and how it would feel. I would shift my mindset into that space so much that it started to feed through into my reality. The way I spoke with customers, my behavior, and my mannerisms all changed to achieve the goal that I set for myself. Try it for yourself and see how you fare.

Having the mindset of always being willing to be the hardest worker in the room and strengthening your own self-awareness will provide us with a consistent level of hard work. In turn, it will show in your day-to-day tasks. Like lifting weights in a gym, working a muscle will help it grow, and the same goes with keeping your composure. Things will trigger your emotional responses, but if you improve these triggers and work on the source of them, over time you'll become accustomed to them and let them wash over you.

Even on public transportation, I would never listen to music or podcasts. I saw the journey as part of the process and didn't want to shy away from the interaction by using headphones or listening to music as an escape. I wanted to be present when it came to what was happening in my surroundings, and I am still the same today. I enjoy being around people and taking on the challenge of being surrounded by different personalities.

Tyson Fury mentioned how he met Wladimir Klitschko in a sauna, years before they fought in the ring. He said how ridiculously hot it was, but he made sure he stayed in longer than Wladimir just to prove a point that he could outwork and take on more stress than him. When Tyson mentioned this to Wladimir in a conference, Wladimir looked bewildered and acted as if it didn't matter, but to Tyson, it did. To some, this may sound crazy, but I think Tyson was right. Those little victories built up his confidence and gave him the mental edge to elevate himself to become a heavyweight champion.

Again, I would envision myself as that top salesperson. I'd imagine the feeling of being number 1. Then, over time, my subconscious and the wiring in my brain would just accept that I was number 1. Then, when opportunities came about to be the top salesperson, I grabbed them with both hands, without fear. My subconscious and mind were already prepped for being in this position, so it never came as a shock.

This may seem like hard work, but the question you need to ask yourself is, "Are my colleagues or competitors doing this?" The answer is probably no. This gives you a resounding edge over them, and it also builds up your resilience and confidence levels as you can handle yourself in stressful situations. The more you're exposed to different environments, the better you'll be able to deal with them and the more confident you'll be. It might sound nice to live in a bubble where nothing ever goes wrong, but in reality, that doesn't happen. Plus, the life skills that are attached to the challenges are invaluable.

If you keep walking away from tough experiences, you'll never learn or grow as a person. Being around all manner of people is a great experience, and the more people you can experience, the better you'll be at handling them. You'll learn how to maneuver around their quirks and traits, and you'll even start to see patterns emerging in certain personalities; it's really quite fascinating! It's amazing how the human condition is programmed to help endure hard times. You may not think you'll be able to complete a certain task, but once you force yourself into that position, you'll be surprised at how well you do. But first, you must make the leap to do it.

Being comfortable with being by yourself and actually allowing it plays a huge part in your success. Once you start to accept yourself, you acknowledge your good and bad points and take them for what they are. Then, through reflection and refinement, you can start to work on the bad points and iron out any imperfections there may be. Once you start to feel more comfortable with yourself, you instantly become more confident and allow your authentic self to shine through. Couple this with having a more agreeable personality trait, and you'll connect with others more easily and build genuine relationships.

A sales floor can be a lonely place, especially if you're number one. It's a dog-eat-dog business, and you have to be able to stand on your own two feet to succeed and provide for your family. All this experience will only help you deal with other people's personalities. You should have a certain selfish streak in sales, and there is nothing wrong with that, but you must have the emotional resistance to tolerate it.

Try spending some time alone to work on yourself spiritually or emotionally, whether that be at home or out going for a walk or taking a class. Not only will your emotional intelligence skyrocket, but you'll also learn to pick up and trust the vibes that your body and being are feeling. This could be difficult to start with, as you may experience different emotions, but by accepting them and dealing with them as they happen, you have a much better chance of being happier and more successful.

Maintaining and nurturing your emotional frequency is essential for success. Be mindful of the people around you, whether you're driving, walking, standing in a line, or taking public transport. There are so many unstable people out there who that aren't in the correct emotional state. It's very easy to get drawn into negativity.

Take driving, for instance; sometimes it's like you need to be two steps ahead of the other drivers to maintain your own peace of mind and safety. By being at the correct frequency and having a clear mind, this comes easily, as you can navigate the potential obstacles that may arise. An example of this is when somebody blatantly cut me off a few years ago, which could have quite easily caused an accident. However, since I was in a present and focused state of mind, I was able to navigate around the driver and continue without incident. I'd compartmentalize the situation that was going on, visualize what I had to do, and then adapt my behavior to maneuver around it without getting upset or angry.

I didn't enter into their emotional turmoil just because they were having a bad day, or acted on impulse because they did; I simply maneuvered around and moved on. Obviously, this would all happen in the span of milliseconds, but this kind of level of focus and clarity is what's also needed to be the top salesperson.

Things will happen that you can't anticipate a shop floor, but maneuvering around them and not reacting is the only way to succeed. My frequency hadn't changed, and even if it had, it would have only gone off kilter slightly, something very easily restored without using much energy. Managing your emotions is so important, in any situation, as it gives you the time and opportunity to think logically, rather than reacting emotionally.

A similar example was a scenario when I was rushing into work one day for some reason and somebody cut me off in the same way. I wasn't in a focused mood, and my frequency was much lower, with thoughts racing around my mind. 56hil time, I lost my composure and pressed the horn. The moment I pressed it, I knew I had failed. Even though I was in the right, that wasn't the point; I'd lost my cool, and my frequency jumped. It took a great deal of effort to get it back to the level where it needed to be in order to sell effectively. I'd also lost momentum. It was my fault for reacting instead of responding, and unfortunately, I paid the price.

I appreciate that these may seem like small scenarios, but in order to be number one, this is the focus and dedication you need to show. Consistently regulating your emotions and not acting on impulse is so important to success.

In sales, not everything is going to go your way. It's a fast-paced environment, and sometimes emotions have the capability to flare. The best salespeople know how to deal with and regulate their emotions, not letting them get the better of them. They get over bad experiences quickly and build resilience.

Recognizing and adapting to other people's personalities and traits is so important, especially in sales. Knowing when to stick or twist, knowing when to engage or stay back—it's all about timing—but one of the most important aspects of sales is to maintain a positive attitude and frequency at all times while maintaining our contained enthusiasm. Once we let our energy spill over, either negatively or positively, it takes a whole lot of work to get back to that original state.

Trust = Surrender & Faith

Trust plays a huge part in sales and is the result of surrendering yourself and having faith in the process.

This is an exercise some salespeople find very difficult: surrendering yourself to someone or something else in the short term. They think this shows a lack of control, but in fact, it's the opposite. Having the foresight to see that showing short-term surrender for the chance of a long-term prize, i.e., a sale and repeated business, is the only way you'll ever be the top salesperson consistently.

Sure, you'll get stung a few times, but that's the compromise. Remember what Shiraz said about falling in love? Having the right frequency also sets the precedent for how your day will go at work. Arriving with a focused mind means you're ready to go. Do you think all of the other salespeople are mindful from the moment they wake up? That they're visualizing their alarm going off the night before? Have they foreseen wearing their uniform before putting it on? Have they anticipated the road rage before it occurred and navigated it correctly? Have they visualized themselves as number one? Will they be in the right frame of mind to expect the unexpected? Just like being the hardest worker in the room, I'd be willing to bet they haven't even given it an afterthought.

Former Mr. Olympia, Dorian Yates, mentioned how he would have to get up and trudge through three feet of snow to get to his gym in Birmingham, England. He'd be annoyed and pissed that his American peers would be in sunny California driving into work in their convertibles. Not only did this make him hungrier to have a stronger workout, but he also mentions how he realized that they weren't doing what he was doing. They weren't going through the torment and sacrifice to achieve their desired outcome, and this gave him the psychological upper hand.

Typical professional salespeople are ruthless by nature and can sniff out weakness in a heartbeat. It's their job to read people, and they're constantly on the lookout for easy prey. That's why you must take it upon yourself to show that you aren't easy prey and that you're actually a force to be reckoned with, a force that is not only willing to compete but to win.

Ensure that the second you walk onto that shop floor, you're at your pinnacle in terms of performance and mindset. Take the time to stop before you enter work and get into the correct frequency. That will help you be the top performer and take on the day. Go into that state of focus. It only takes a few seconds, but it works. Under no circumstances should you go running in like a headless chicken or with your head in the clouds. Every thought and every fiber of your body must be committed to giving that day your very best effort while still being in a positive emotional state.

In many of the retail stores I worked in, we operated split shifts. There was always an early shift and a late shift. The early shift was obviously there from early morning and left at a more normal closing hour, such as 5 or 6 p.m., whereas a late shift started a little later, say around 11 a.m. or noon, and stayed until the store closed.

The issue I had with the late shifts was that getting in a few hours after everybody else always threw me off my game. The dynamics of the salespeople had already been set, and the atmosphere was in their favor. Obviously, walking into that atmosphere was hard. Getting involved was hard, as I was the outsider. The salespeople who were in already had their own system for how the day was going and how customers were being served. Not only did I struggle to fit in, but the other salespeople didn't want me to fit in! The more mouths at the table, the more there is to feed!

That's why, whenever I was working a late shift, I would always make sure I was in when the store opened, or at the very latest, just after. This made sure I was involved in the goings-on on the shop floor and had my equal share of customers throughout the day. I didn't get paid for the two extra hours that I worked, but I did get to keep the commission on the product I sold. Plus, I was in the right mentality to sell all day; win-win, right?

Obviously, this depends on where you work and whether this would be allowed by the management team. Still, even if you could just go in early to get the admin and paperwork side of the job completed before you started your day, you'd be in a better position, leaving you with more time for sales. I would never work on my days off, as I didn't feel there was a need to, but what I did do was maximize every single hour of the days that I did work. That ensured I wasn't in a position where I had to work on days off. The way I figured it, if I worked hard through the week and booked what I did, I earned my days off.

Chapter 4

Entering Work & Starting the Day

I'd arrive at work and make sure my tools were set up for the day. I needed to have at least two pens, a calculator, and a piece of paper for working things out on my person before anything else. This made sure I was prepared for the day ahead. All of these little victories made me even more confident.

It goes without saying that your mobile phone needs to be put away too, doesn't it? Either put it in a safe or in a locker so you can't access it easily. Mobile phones are one of the biggest distractions of the modern era and will take away your focus and confidence in an instant. I read once that studies show that it takes upwards of 20 minutes to get back into the state of focus you were in before you checked your phone. That's crazy! All for the sake of checking Instagram or Facebook. This is also another example of not acting on impulse. Just because you have a craving to check your Messenger or Instagram account doesn't mean you need to. When you control that craving and mentally say no, you'll feel more confident and disciplined in your approach. Try it and see if it works for you.

We've all seen it when we go into a store or restaurant. The server is on their phone, and it's not a good look. Yes, many salespeople say that this is obvious stuff, which it absolutely is!

How many can honestly say that they leave their phone unattended until dinner or at home? Can you?

Being in the moment is so important, as we have to channel all of our focus into the task at hand. If we're not focused or at 100%, we won't inspire customers enough to trust us and make the purchase. If anybody needs to call you for an emergency, they'll ring the store. Under no circumstances would I stand at the water fountain or coffee machine gossiping about the latest news or discussing pointless negative topics. There's nothing that kills positivity more than negative people or situations, so please stay out of their way.

What would be the point of clearing your mind and getting into the right frequency to have a fantastic day at work, only to stand around gossiping to John or Sally? Or, to enter into conversations about how somebody didn't do something they should have, and how bad they are for it. I know this may be a hard behavior to get out of, but this sets the benchmark and the precedent for the day. Whilst everybody else is gossiping at the back of the store, you've got your mind on the customers that could, and will, be walking in from the front of the store, easy pickings, right?

I'd then get straight onto a computer to complete the admin tasks that I had set for myself in the days prior. This could be ordering samples, chasing suppliers for products, or following up with customers that I have spoken to before. Sometimes I'd even handle the odd complaint or service issue. I would get through this task as quickly as possible while still not rushing the process; I'd just work more efficiently. Every second that I was doing the paperwork side of the job was a second less on the sales floor. Obviously, nobody wants to do the boring admin side of the work, but unfortunately, it comes as part and parcel. By ensuring it's completed first thing and allocating that time to do it without rushing or acting impulsively, we can then have a clear mind for the day ahead of selling. Unless it was extremely quiet in the afternoon, I would never do administrative work of any kind. I would always set aside time in the morning to complete all paperwork and phone calls to make sure the rest of the day was clear.

Under no circumstances should you ignore your admin work. The longer you leave tasks that need to be completed, the more stress and anxiety you will feel. This will affect your frequency and mentality, as you'll know you're behind and lose confidence and momentum. If you told somebody that you would call them, then you must call them, regardless of the conversation. It's the ability to have these hard conversations that makes us stronger and more resilient. We tend to avoid behaviors and interactions like this because we don't want to hear the outcome, as there is potential for them to end badly.

If we just keep sticking our heads in the sand, we just end up with antagonized customers and a negative state of mind. By taking charge of the situation, we can be proactive in our approach, and naturally, we'll start looking for possible solutions. I would treat my order book as my own business, and the customers I had served were my responsibility. I appreciate that I had a manager, but in my eyes, the buck stopped with me. I was accountable for my actions and, ultimately, the amount of commission I earned. Closing more orders meant I earned more commission, but I also had more responsibility.

Let's say a customer was complaining about a product and wanted their money back. Ignoring that customer will only annoy them further and send the situation past the point of reconciliation. But by speaking with customers directly and showing that we care about their issues, we instantly elevate our standing as the credible leader that we made ourselves out to be at the point of sale; we'll be more competent in the eyes of the customer. Nine times out of ten, customers don't actually want their money back on products, even if they say they do. They just want the product they bought under the conditions they bought it under. By staying calm and letting the customer vent their frustration, you help diffuse the situation and leave them in a better position to receive the solution from you.

Say a customer ordered a new sofa, and the frame collapsed after only a few weeks. They'd obviously call you or come into the store to discuss why it happened and how it's going to be fixed. That's more than a reasonable request, as sofas can cost a lot of money, and they've placed their trust in you as the salesperson as well as the company. Don't then be annoyed or upset that you must deal with them. Even if it's a weekend and there are 100 other customers in the store, you should still show that customer the courtesy and professionalism shown through the prior sales process. The entire customer experience is a process, and if the relationship is damaged at this point, what will the customer think?

This won't result in repeat business or recommendations. Most people will be reasonable, provided they can see that something is being done to rectify the issue. When they explain the issue, show empathy and slightly shake your head. Raise your eyebrows in genuine shock when the customer explains what is wrong with the product or service, while still keeping your enthusiasm contained. Visualize what the customer is saying to you, imagine the issue arising, and instantly think of the solution. Don't get dragged into their emotional turmoil; instead, remain logical. Never interject with a solution. Always let them get their grievances off their chest after sympathizing with them.

Always sincerely apologize when you're in the wrong. An apology goes a long way, and showing that vulnerability helps a customer feel valued and understood. We then go full throttle into sorting the problems out for them. Explain how you'll rectify the issue, if it can be, and how you are on top of it until it is.

Say things like, "I get your position and feel what you're going through. Leave it with me, and I promise I'll stay on top of this until the matter is solved. I'm sorry for the inconvenience and shall call you when we have moved things forward," or other related phrases. This takes the sting out of the customers' experience, and they'll leave you to sort out the issue, as they've trusted you enough to follow through. Often times, I would simply tell the customer, "You just want your sofa the way you bought it," when they originally came in for a refund. All I had to do was listen to their position and act as their councilor for a few minutes. Sometimes that's all people need—somebody to take their frustration out on for a few seconds.

If you can't handle this, just remember the long game of the conversation. If the refund is given, you'll lose the figures from your quota and the commission too. You need to be on the same emotional frequency as them to deal with their issues correctly. More importantly, make the customer feel like they're valued and that their business matters, because it does. Surrender to their position and have an attitude of, "Something isn't right, so let's sort it out now."

I think my experience working in my brother's shop at such a young age helped me be like this. If I didn't carry out the tasks, I was either asked why I hadn't done them, or nobody dealt with them because there was nobody else to do them. By dealing with the issues yourself and not just passing them along to your manager, you will have a greater sense of confidence and assertiveness. Really own your customers and your client base. Treat your order book as if it were your mini-business, because that's exactly what it is. If you treat your customers with the same respect and decency you'd want to be treated with, they'll keep coming back to you.

There are times, however, when customers will not relent and you can't appease them. Only at this point of making sure you can honestly say you can't do anymore for them personally should you ask a manager to step in and help. Once the manager is dealing with them, go back to your business and carry on doing whatever you were doing. Once you know the manager has a good handle on it, then have the freedom and confidence to get on with your work.

There are a minority of people who will stand arguing about an issue and will not relent, regardless of the solutions you give them. I would say the majority of these people are purely there for a discount of some sort, and to save any future disagreements, I'd give them one. It's worth the 5–15% you give back to not have an angry customer or negative review on social media.

If it's busy, when appropriate, after you've acknowledged the customers' issues and acknowledged their pain, mention how you'll sort the issues out and that they'll hear from somebody in the next few days. I would then suggest you schedule the call for the next morning and complete whatever procedure is necessary pertaining to what was discussed with the customer.

The idea is for you to spend as much time on the shop floor as possible and be available to customers. I would never promise or tell a customer something that I wouldn't have to be involved in. If there was a service department, I would mention how the service department would get back to them. If I were ordering samples, I would tell them I will order the samples and get them sent. I wouldn't call them to let them know I'd done it; I'd just do it, make a note in the diary or their paperwork that I had, then go about my day selling. Obviously, if ordering a sample was for future business, then I would have set a reminder in my diary to give them a call in 2-3 days and discuss whether they had received the sample, how it looked in their room, and if they'd made a decision.

Following up is so important, but hardly anybody ever does it. Especially in retail, once the hard work is more or less done, it's just about finalizing the order. Not to mention if the customer has placed an order subject to color, something we'll discuss later as a closing technique. If the customers haven't received the samples, let them know that you'll order them some more, order them again, and give them another call in 2-3 days.

You can always judge a company or salesperson by the after-sales tasks that occur. It's all very well and good being fantastic upfront, promising everything to the customer, and saying how it'll all be perfect. Potential issues arise when promises aren't kept. Whether or not you follow through will show your real character.

This isn't to say that when completing admin work, you completely ignore customers on the shop floor. If a customer walks into the store or the phone rings, you serve them, as money will always come first. Just remember that the admin work must be done every day to your best ability in order to win and keep the momentum flowing.

Whenever I was on the shop floor, I was always hungry and ready to serve customers. Regardless of how big or small my target was, my mindset was always the same. There are different ways that sales targets are created, and here is a method that I believe is both fair and effective. It considers the fact that sale days such as Saturdays, Sundays, and bank holidays are busier than normal days of the week, thus increasing the amount a consultant should be able to book. A normal day would be worth 1 point, whereas a sale day would be worth 2 points.

First, you should work out how much 1 point would be. Simply add together all of the points worked and then divide that by the total store target. Here is the work schedule for the six sales professionals in the store:

John: Monday, Tuesday, Wednesday, Thursday, Friday - 5 Points

Alan: Monday, Wednesday, Friday, Saturday, Sunday - 7 Points

Josie: Wednesday, Thursday, Friday, Saturday, Sunday - 7 Points

Jim: Monday, Tuesday, Friday, Saturday, Sunday - 7 Points

Sam: Wednesday, Thursday, Friday, Saturday, Sunday - 7 Points

Lorenzo: Monday, Tuesday, Wednesday, Thursday, Saturday - 6 Points

Total: 39 Points

Now let's say that the store target was $200,000 for the week. This would be divided by 39, giving you the total amount per point: 200,000/39 = 5,128.20

Let's round it up to 5,150 to make it even. Then you'd multiply 5,150 by the number of points somebody has in a week. John, for instance, has 5 points, so his target would be $25,750. Have a look at the graph below to see how this works.

	Mon	Tues	Wed	Thurs	Fri	Sat	Sun	Total
John	$5150	$5150	$5150	$5150	$5150	Day off	Day off	$25,750
Alan	$5150	Day off	$5150	Day off	$5150	$10,300	$10,300	$36,050
Josie	Day off	Day off	$5150	$5150	$5150	$10,300	$10,300	$36,050
Jim	$5150	$5150	Day off	Day off	$5150	$10,300	$10,300	$36,050
Sam	$5150	$5150	Day off	Day off	$5150	$10,300	$10,300	$36,050
Lorenzo	$5150	$5150	$5150	$5150	Day off	$10,300	Day off	$30,900

The issue is that most salespeople believe that if they have a quiet week, they'll make it all back on the weekend. Sometimes, they'll take a laidback approach during the week. What if the weekend wasn't as busy as they had hoped? This would almost certainly mean that their target wouldn't be achieved, and they would fall into the negative.

I would always split my total weekly target into the days I was working and not take note of whether they were sale days or not. My target in this instance would have been $36,050. I would set my own personal daily target of $7,210. This meant that if I achieved this target during the 3 days I worked during the week, I would be ahead of my total percentage for the week coming into the weekend.

This meant I had a huge head start since chances were that the weekend would be busier and I would have had my target booked by Saturday night or Sunday morning at the latest. This left me with the remainder of my time to start booking for next week's target. This is how I always remained well above the target I was given. Even though I had achieved my quota early, I'd never stop or slow down. I'd keep the momentum going and just keep booking whatever was in front of me.

This also put me in a great position for when the inevitable dry weeks came. In sales, there will always be weeks where nobody seems to buy or nobody walks through the door; it happens. By having this backup of banked orders, even if I missed my week, the chances were I never missed my target because the other weeks helped carry me over. Just because other people aren't as hungry as you doesn't mean that you have to take your foot off the gas. Keep going even during those lull periods, because they could provide that sale that may save you from a hard meeting with your sales manager. Forget about the politics; rise above them. Do what's best for you.

Never be intimidated by your target. A target is relative to the advertising and marketing budget set by the company. Once the January sales start, the targets are normally higher; this isn't just by chance. This is because traditionally, these are the busiest periods, and this is where most of the advertising budget is being spent. If there is more advertising taking place, there will be more customers walking through the door. When your company isn't in a promotion or sale period, the targets are lower in most cases. This is because there are fewer advertising and marketing costs.

This is when the true salespeople come alive, because it's difficult to sell to people who aren't necessarily coming in because they've seen or heard an offer on TV or radio. Salespeople must find that extra grit to dig deep and really work for that order, as there are no extra promotions or incentives for customers to buy. This is a perfect example of doing what nobody else does; the majority of salespeople will write off this period, as it won't make much difference to your annual target if you don't hit it. However, I believe it absolutely does, as it affects your mindset, mentality, and attitude towards work. This would be another example of "kicking the can down the road." By doing the little things right, momentum is gained and confidence is created. You're ready for the customers to walk through the door.

Double Your Sales Through Referrals

Ok, guys, let's take a break from the sales side for a second. Let's discuss how you can get more customers to come to you personally without busting your guts! I want you to go out and buy 10 x A5 plastic leaflet racks—you know, the plastic holders on the side of desks? Then, I want you to buy some evergreen leaflets. There should be no dates or time constraints on them. Go to your local business where your perfect avatar would visit.

Who is your perfect avatar? Is it young couples? Maybe it's an older generation? Affluent professionals? Based on that information, list a place where these people will go. Restaurants, gyms, independent stores, food halls, etc. Then, go into those places and suggest that they act as paid affiliates for you or your company. If they give a leaflet out to every one of their customers, for everyone that comes into your store and buys, mention to them how you'll pay them a percentage of the sale.

Extra for experts: the best way to do this is to make the sales assistants eager. Make them want to give the leaflets out. The tried and tested method for doing this is to recommend that all the money earned be saved until the end of the year, and their Christmas party will be paid for by you! The team members love this, as the more customers they recommend, the better party they have. Code or stamp the back of the leaflets so you know where they've come from and keep a running total of the finances. Mention on the POS how if they bring in the leaflet and purchase from you or your company directly, the customers also receive a free gift, such as a bottle of wine, a box of chocolates, etc. The leaflets should be given out in correlation with any sales you have. You may have to call them at the start of every month to let them know. While on the phone, let them know how much commission your best affiliate has earned to stoke their fire and create a little competition. Alternatively, two months of giving and one month of not giving work just as well. If you can find ten establishments that will facilitate this, you'll be well on your way to doubling your sales with half the stress in two years or less. Guaranteed!

Every year I take a select few students and help them Double Your Sales With Half The Stress In 2 Years Or Less, Guaranteed. Seventy-five percent of the fee is linked to results. Fair enough?

If you'd like to apply, see if you'd be a good fit. Contact me by the means below:

info@fromfeartomindful.com

www.linkedin.com/in/sam-king-from-fear-to-mindful/

I also offer a great referral incentive to anyone who refers a salesperson or company that may benefit from this program and gets through the application process.

Chapter 5

Knowledge Is Power

Salespeople must be absolutely knowledgeable about the products they're selling, as they're meant to be authority figures. If a customer feels that they know more about a certain product than the salesperson, then the chances are they will never buy from them. Even if they do, it will only be because they're in a desperate position or were already certain to be buying in the first place. It's just an awkward exchange, isn't it?

If you're new to the job, then you shouldn't be expected to know everything. However, you should learn as you go along. Never be afraid to serve customers just because you don't know every little detail about a certain product. If a question comes up that you're unsure of, simply admit this to the customer, along with an explanation that you're new. Tell them you'll find out for them. This honesty will go a long way, and they'll appreciate you for it. It also gives you an objection you can proactively overcome next time.

Is there anything you're unsure of in your store? Perhaps when you have a period of downtime, you should research the details. This makes you a stronger salesperson for the next customer who comes in to buy.

Ensnare Their Senses

Let your customers be greeted with the amazing smell of new products and fresh coffee. This will set the benchmark for a homely greeting, making them feel comfortable enough to buy. I heard that orange zest is one of the best fragrances to get the creative juices flowing! Perhaps room fresheners near the door would help with this!

Don't Jump Out at Them!

Never shout from the other side of the building or pounce on them the second they walk through the door. This will only raise their sales resistance and make it harder for you to meet their needs and desires. Instead, welcome them graciously into your store. Always center yourself and clear your mind before any interaction. Pure openness and transparency are key to helping with this, no matter the pressure you're under. Giving off an almost laissez-faire attitude only draws people more to your presence, but remember, inside you're as sharp as a tack.

This is a warm market, and we aren't cold callers ringing people or knocking on doors. Customers have come of their own accord, so chances are we don't have to *sell* anything, so advising in a consultant role is always the best method. People are programmed to be wary of salespeople, so it's our job to lower their guard.

I'll give you an example of how I got the "Meet & Greet" part absolutely wrong. I was working a few years ago in a large store selling flooring, and there were no customers in the store. We, the salespeople, were talking amongst ourselves. This was wrong anyway, as we shouldn't have been congregating in groups. It's unsightly and can be quite intimidating for the customer. Imagine walking in and seeing a group of salespeople staring at you; it's like a firing squad!

Anyway, a lady came walking quite fast into the store, and I just flat out asked her, "Hello, were you looking for anything in particular?" I had no interest in how her frequency was or what state she was in; I wasn't mindful of my words, actions, or tonalities. In fact, I forced out the words instead of articulating them properly, letting them roll out. The lady turned around to me and very abruptly said, "A f***ing hoover!" Note that a hoover is a vacuum cleaner. She then spun around and left the store. I was in absolute shock.

Obviously, as you can imagine, the entire sales team was in hysterics, as I'd just been put in my place. That was fair enough, but joking aside, that customer came into the store for a reason. Yes, she came in with a rushed attitude. Yes, she may not have been in the best state of mind to make a sizeable purchase. So what? It was my job to serve that customer to the best of my ability, regardless of her attitude, and I wasn't sensitive enough to her needs. If I'd have just spent a split second to calm my mind and adjust my frequency, there would have been a possibility that she could have spent thousands.

Saying hello, or at a minimum, acknowledging the entire entourage, is a must too, not just the person who you believe to be the decision-maker. Remember, people are making a decision that will impact their entire family. Therefore, all family members should be included in the process, whether they be children, parents, in-laws, aunties, or uncles.

In some cultures, making decisions must be done by the whole family. I've dealt with many Asian families when selling sofas, and they have brought along their aunties and uncles to have an opinion and be involved. When I've explained why a certain leather is better than the other and how it will benefit them, or any other feature or benefit, I've made eye contact and explained it to that auntie or uncle as well, not just the person with the purse strings. I made them feel involved in the process because they were involved. They were here taking part in the same conversation, and that's why they had to feel like they mattered.

Obviously, I wouldn't have spoken primarily to the auntie or uncle; I'd still be speaking predominantly to the decision-makers, but every now and then I'd throw a comment or gesture towards the auntie or uncle to ensure they felt involved. This complete openness and transparency only enhanced my credibility and trust with the customers. Not only this, but the auntie and uncle may, at some point, need a sofa. Who are they more likely to go to? That strange salesperson who runs the risk of them being "sold to," or that friendly salesperson who made them feel included that time when shopping with their niece or nephew? I think you know the answer.

As horrible as it sounds, I would never intentionally interact with children that were at a "temperamental" age. I suppose this is debatable, but I'd say definitely up to the ages of 8 or 9, I would try my utmost to not interact with them. This is purely due to the fact that if they were behaving well and everything was fine, I didn't want to do anything to change that. Interacting could only open a can of annoyed children, which could then turn into a family leaving because they were making a scene. I'd never be cold towards anybody, but this is just the way I operated. Once the sale had been finalized, I'd shake the child's hand and get them a drink. But that's as far as it went. If a child was pleasant and friendly, I'd reciprocate, but I wouldn't go out of my way for a connection.

I've seen in some retail stores now that they've installed a small, enclosed play pen for their customers' children. What an amazing idea to keep them entertained while their parents shop! Sure, it might take up a few square feet of space, but if you could designate a zone on your floor to have a few books and toys available for would-be sale killers, it's worth a shot, isn't it?

Come into Their World at Their Level

Take a second to note how the customers are walking in, mark them in your mind, and align yourself with the frequency they're at. If they look like they're taking their time, then gracefully welcome them to the store in a warm, yet slightly assertive, soft tone, matching their frequency. If they're looking to be in a bit more of a rush, welcome them slightly more assertively while matching their tonality. Always come into the customer's world on their level. Never try to slow down or hurry up a customer; it'll only confuse and antagonize them.

You become so much more relatable and easier to get along with. This lowers sales resistance and increases the chances of people telling you their needs and wants.

By matching your frequency to theirs, you'll see and feel when somebody is either interested or disinterested in a product based on their natural reactions. The more you fine-tune your empathy, the easier it'll be to spot the signals.

Try to be more enthusiastic than them; you come across as pushy, raising sales resistance. Try to be slightly less enthusiastic than them; you will come across as not interested in the sale or, worse, manipulative.

It's our job to adapt to the customer, not the other way around. By using empathy, we can judge the emotions and frequencies of others. Very often, people believe that empathy means feeling sorry for other people; however, this isn't the case. Empathy means the ability to understand and share the feelings of another.

How to Address Customers

Whenever I would speak to a customer, I would talk as if they were an esteemed colleague: with respect, but it also allowed me to be my true self. The more you're able to express your true, genuine self while still being professional, the more a customer will trust you, and your level of rapport will strengthen. I would, however, when writing up an invoice, ask for their names and call them Mr. or Mrs. X. This will maintain the right level of respect between you and maintain the sales-customer relationship. Of course, there are some customers you can be more casual with than others, but having the empathy and emotional awareness to read these situations is a must to stay in rapport and not look foolish.

I remember once serving a quite well-to-do woman who had come back in for another look at a product. Here's how the conversation went:

Me: "Nice to see you again!"

Customer: "Oh, you remember me?"

Me: "Of course, I always remember the bad ones!"

Now, this was said in a fun and jokey way, which was not intended to cause offense in any form, but it did. Needless to say, she didn't buy from me then or ever when she came into the store. If I had not acted on impulse because I was under pressure and had come into her world on her frequency, I'd have been much more composed to have a conversation that would have had a more positive result.

Answering The Telephone

Something as simple as answering the telephone in the correct manner can make a huge difference in your relationship with your customer. Similar to greeting and speaking with them face-to-face, always answer in a composed manner and center yourself before any interaction. I'll talk more about this in the next few chapters. This allows you and the customer to seamlessly have a conversation that serves them rather than taking them aback with a disgruntled or abrupt greeting.

A perfect greeting when answering the telephone would be: "Thanks for calling 'Company Y,' John speaking; how can I help?"

Greeting the Customer

There are so many greetings that typical salespeople use, but many are pointless as either they increase sales resistance or everyone uses them, so they become cliché. Here are some typical greetings:

"Hi, how are you? How can I help you?"

"Good morning. Can I help you?"

"Good afternoon, were you looking for anything in particular?"

"Morning, madam, here are some special offers we have today."

While some customers will tell you their innermost wants and needs, the vast majority will give you those dreaded words salespeople don't want to hear: "Just looking."

This is because every single salesperson in the world uses these kinds of greetings. So, when you use them, it makes you a typical salesperson that nobody wants to deal with. The second they hear the usual greeting, their guards are up, and sales resistance is high. There is a chance of bringing this down during the sales process, but from my own experience, it's difficult. First impressions count, and as this is the first verbal interaction you'll have, you must make it a good one.

If not, you'll start to lose the ability to influence the conversation. When you ask a question and don't get the answer you're looking for or are shut down, you're not seen as the authority figure. You'll lose your confidence, and the energy has been lost. You can get the sale back, but it's difficult. The best salespeople however always dig deep enough and have the resilience to find a way to get the energy back. It's easier however to make it seamless from the get-go, regardless of the customer's attitude.

As sales professionals, it's our job to work around this psychology so you get the answer you want. This is what the best salespeople do: they get their answer to their question, regardless of what's unfolding in front of them. The meet and greet is so important, as it sets a benchmark for the customer's experience and the relationship between the two of you. Customers come into a store in a defensive manner. It's our job to relieve them of this pressure and make their experience easier and more satisfying, while being as efficient as possible and extracting the information we need to create a sale without the customer feeling as if we were intrusive. Nobody is ever just looking; this is just the go-to phrase that people use to ward off "sharky" salespeople.

The number of times I've converted a "just looker" into a buyer by using the following greeting is off the charts. Never let your spirits be dampened because somebody says they're just looking, and never believe that that's the truth. More often than not, it isn't. Many people ask me how to lower sales resistance and get customers to open up more easily. The best greeting I can ever recommend to avoid customer resistance is: "Hi guys, are you just looking or are you looking for something in particular?"

You can change the wording if you wish, but ensure the structure is the same. Greet them, ask if they're just looking, and then proceed to help them. As long as it comes across in a genuine, cool, and friendly way with love, it will endear people to your personality, and the chances of them opening up straight away increase tenfold.

This greeting completely disarms the objection and puts the customer on the back foot. Most times, people would reveal and explain what they were looking for. I would then delve into their why factor, finding out as much as I could without being pushy. Some questions on how to find people's whys are on the following pages.

An ideal greeting would be, "Hi guys, welcome to the store. Are you just looking, or are you looking for something in particular?"

The issue I found with this, however, was that most customers feared walking into a store, and the mere greeting of "Welcome to the store" would raise resistance and make them say they were just looking. It goes without saying that you should disarm the customer of these words before they say them; that's why I would be slightly shorter in my approach. Try it and see what works for you in the environment you're in.

Sometimes customers were slightly taken back by this greeting and didn't really know how to handle it; some were even a little defensive by the question and replied in a manner such as, "We'll shout if we need anything." Some would even be sarcastic and reply, "A carpet" or "A sofa." I would reply, "Yeah, anything in particular?" and look at them with a warm smile, as if to carry on with the conversation and let the energy flow. I would never let a negative encounter like this dampen my spirits, as I made it the customer's choice to either give me the information I needed to serve them or not.

I was never the one to break away from this interaction. If I did, I wouldn't be seen as the authority, and the customers wouldn't have had a reason to trust me because I was weak, even if I was still emitting a warm and pleasant vibe. If they did give me a dismissive answer such as "We'll shout if we need anything," I would never be offended or defensive. I'd simply say "sure" or "no worries," with a smile. I'd also give them a non-offensive hand gesture to insinuate that I was of no harm to them, and they were more than welcome to look in their own time and at their own pace.

You could say something along the lines of "Sure, I'll leave it with you." But you must make sure this is in a genuine caring tonality rather than a passive aggressive one to keep sales resistance low.

As salespeople, we must be the sponge that takes that resistance, if and when there is any, from the interaction rather than fueling it. This ensures the process runs seamlessly, and therefore, we should be extremely delicate with the words we articulate, especially in such a crucial and sensitive part of the sales process as first impressions. They are everything, and it draws people into our gravitas rather than repelling them.

Some would tell me without hesitation and point out the exact model or description of what they wanted. Some would look at each other, if they were a couple, and say to each other, "Shall we just...?" as if to say, "Shall we just put our trust in this person and let them know what we want?"

I would even use this greeting if a customer was clearly settled on a product and the chances of them buying were high, rather than steamrolling in expecting an order. This allowed the customer to adjust and come to terms with the fact that a salesperson was on hand to help them, not just take an order. This lowered sales resistance even further, and many times I got a response such as, "I think we've found what we're looking for."

When customers make statements like this, they're clearly nearly ready to buy. Still, don't take this as a given, or you can end up running the risk of turning confidence into arrogance by overspilling your enthusiasm. I was watching a documentary about veterans of World War I. They interviewed many soldiers that were on the frontline, and they all discussed how horrendous it was. They all mentioned how the conditions were terrible and that it was the worst time of their lives, apart from one.

One man was asked how he felt about the experiences he had witnessed during the numerous battles he'd seen, and he replied how he thought they were: "All such a lot of fun." This man had been on the frontlines of arguably the worst war in history and seen things that aren't imaginable, and that was his response? I was dumbfounded.

At the end of the show, it produced a reel of what all the brave gentlemen did for work after the war. Some were bricklayers, some were taxi drivers, some were managers, and some were even business owners. Then came the turn of the man, who seemed almost upbeat about his time during the war. "Mr. X" went on to have a fantastic career in sales and marketing.

I couldn't help but laugh. This man was the absolute essence of what every salesperson should be. He lived in trenches, was shot at, probably saw many of his friends and colleagues injured or worse, and that's how he responded. What a guy.

This sheer positive outlook on life and resilience are what make the best salespeople. By never letting yourself get down about a situation, you'll make sure you're ready and able to transfer that much-needed energy to the next customer you'll be serving, increasing the chances of them trusting you and opening up to you.

For an extra free resource on this technique, visit https://www.fromfeartomindful.com/resources/.

Don't Rush It

Slow down when talking to customers, especially in the first interaction. Very often, salespeople, myself included, speak way too fast when interacting with people, and they can't comprehend what's being said. This can only confuse people and instantly raise their barrier of resistance. Have you ever noticed that when you speak to a customer in an unthoughtful or flippant manner they instantly answer with something defensive? If you slow down your speech and really mean and articulate the words you're saying with energy and purpose, they'll have more time to acknowledge and digest every little detail of what you've just said.

Channel your anxiety and energy down using the breathing techniques in "Setting the Stage: Part 2 (Added Bonus)."

This experience is new to them, and the chances are that they don't know the common knowledge of products and services that you do. It will be a lot to take in the first time around. Try to be sensitive to that.

Building Rapport

Rapport isn't created by just a single act that you do to check a box. It's an ongoing exercise that is constantly being built. Many people think that finding one common ground or giving a mindless compliment instantly means that you're in rapport and they now have the divine right to sell you anything they want, which isn't the case.

Say, for instance, that a man walked into a store with a nice hat on. I'd never make a comment about it. Why? Chances are that somebody else made that comment, and therefore my comment would be just another comment. If I really liked the hat, I would more than likely mention it, but only at the end of the sale when writing up the order, because I knew that the sale was in the bag and we had built up a strong enough relationship to do so. It would come across and be accepted as genuine.

Actively listening to somebody is one of the biggest compliments you can give. People love to talk about themselves, and when it's a one-way conversation in their favor, they normally feel great about the person who was on the other side listening to them. Let people talk, and as long as you actively listen and delve deeper into their subject, a stronger connection will be created naturally. If you then show them relative products that fit the description or problems they've just explained, they'll respect and appreciate you more because you're looking out for their best interests. They'll start to realize you're trustworthy, and they can count on you and your expertise.

Now you're starting to be seen as a professional authority that is efficient and succinct. Customers are busy people, the less amount of time and energy they spend in your store, the better. The majority of people don't want to be shopping for new items any more than they have to, so don't waste their time with flippant comments.

Often the golden nuggets of information are found in the quips of the conversation, or perhaps in the part where the customer doesn't feel like it's as big a deal as it could be. It could be a game-changer. This is why always being attentive to what the customer says is so important. Don't cut them short; it's standard practice to be polite too.

If your talking is taking up over 40% of the conversation at this stage, then unfortunately, you're doing it wrong. Remember the old saying about how you've got two ears and one mouth? Allow the customer to explain their situation to you without interrupting them or losing your contained enthusiasm. Keep it bubbling away. To listen well, you may need to restrain yourself from disagreeing, interjecting, giving advice, or talking about your own experience—temporarily, at least.

You have two ears and one mouth, remember?

"Listening is a one-sided relationship."
- Michael Nichols

People can tell whether you're interested in a subject or not from the subconscious and natural reactions that you make. These reactions aren't controllable, even for the best of liars! When a subject comes up that you genuinely enjoy, your eyes light up naturally, and you speak with more excitement.

Take your time with such conversations. If a customer starts talking about a different subject, converse with them about it showing an interest in their opinions and views. If you have a thoughtful comment or are curious about a subject and wish to delve deeper into said subject, lean in on it. This will deepen rapport and strengthen the relationship as long as you always keep the focus on your customer and share their experiences in a positive light. This is so important, it's as equally as important as the 'sales' process as people will warm to you and for reasons we've mentioned above. As far as I'm concerned, this is the sales process. Here sometimes the finer details come to fruition that could make a big difference in the decision making. Always keep your ears open for any information that could help you serve them with their product or service choices. It also opens up opportunities for more information that could be thoughtfully extracted to make future sales at a later date. Always bring these thoughts up after so not to come across as pushy.

Always let the conversation run its course through the customers' eyes. When they're finished with a conversation, let it end and drift back to the sale. This has to be on their terms. It's their experience, their money and therefore we have to be willing to go to that place to accommodate them.

I know it's difficult, especially when there is sales pressure from targets or managers. Even more so when its a busy sale day but taking the time to ground yourself and be fully present with your customer and client, almost ignoring all else that is happening in the world will pay dividends. Many salespeople aren't doing this and are leaving so much money table. Even if they get the sale, it wouldn't have been as much as it could have plus, the relationship won't be as strong meaning less referrals in the future.

The best salespeople are the ones who are curious and inquisitive. It's not necessarily being nosey; they have a genuine interest in most things. Some salespeople can get too inquisitive, though, especially when the store is busy. If there is a store full of customers to serve and you're talking about how lovely a certain country is or how interesting a hobby is, there will be a lot of customers left unserved, resulting in a loss of revenue and commission. Even if the store is empty, I still wouldn't get into a full-blown conversation about a subject, as we need to loop the conversation back to the sale. If we don't, customers will end up forgetting the reason why they came into the store, and you'll run the risk of losing the sale.

I was serving a customer and their family of three generations with an expensive sofa a few years ago, and they decided it was for them. They had mentioned earlier in the sale that they were interested in a dining suite too, so I invited them to have a look upstairs after they made the decision. They did and found a table that was nearly up to par, but it wasn't quite ticking all of their boxes. I knew it wasn't for them, even though they stood discussing it for quite some length. I could feel that the customers' concentration was dwindling, and as time went on, I even felt like they were talking themselves out of the entire sale.

I could see their minds drifting, as there were a few opinions within the group going back and forth. They mentioned how they were going to think about it and come back since they were undecided. This was fine, but I felt the sofa slip from my grip. I said it assertively. but not aggressively, in a lower tone: "You're still having the sofa, right?"

They all looked at each other as if to say, "I'd completely forgotten about that!" They agreed to buy the sofa. This is a perfect example of keeping your mind on the topic and purpose of the conversation. You have to be that constant that brings people back to the reason they're with you: to buy. Of course, this has to be done in a subtle and sincere manner, as we don't want to upset anybody or raise resistance, but we must remember the reason why we're at work.

Whether that is for providing a better future for our families, buying luxury items, bigger houses to live in, or making investments for the future. Maybe you're just very competitive and want to be the top dog in your store, which is fair enough. They're the real reasons we go to work, but providing great service is how we sustain our dreams and make them a reality for the long-term. It also keeps our mental and emotional well-being intact, as we stay reasonable people rather than sharky salespeople, lying or using people just to get ahead. The better the service we provide, the more money we make. Rapport is a result of actions that lead to a customer trusting you. Rapport builds over hours, days, months, and years. The stronger you fall into rapport, the stronger the chance of repeat business, and the easier it is to make more sales.

Think of sales as a business, and the customers are in your funnel. A very poor salesperson would only think of the here and now when booking business and not have the capacity or foresight to acknowledge that some customers take longer to make decisions. If a customer keeps coming into a store to look at a product, they're showing signs that someday they'll buy it. They must still be served correctly from a professional standpoint, but it puts us in front of their minds when they are ready to buy. The second we ignore a customer or dismiss them as time-wasters, we lose rapport. Our energy has diminished, and the sale and relationship are over. These are very few and far between, as most people want to get their purchases made and out of the way, but some do like to take their time and make decisions over weeks or months. We have to accommodate that.

The classic *How to Win Friends and Influence People*—as good as it is—I disagree with one point that was made. Although it was said in a different context than retail sales, it mentions how to flatter somebody before an interaction and pay them compliments so they interact with you in a more positive manner. Personally, I think this is a bad idea and have never practiced it, especially in a retail sales setting. Most people in this day and age can spot fake compliments and will instantly recognize the hidden agenda. What about you? Do you recognize when somebody is being a little too nice for their own good? Have you ever felt it come across as almost pushy or covert?

Always play the long game with sales. We're not looking for a quick fix or trying to dupe the customer into buying something. We must genuinely want what's best for the customer, even if that means reluctantly telling them that you don't have the product they need. When you do this, you'll be held in higher esteem in the customers' eyes because you're a person who tells them straight. You aren't somebody who just tells them what they want to hear to just get a sale. Just a side note: if this is the case, this is a perfect opportunity to ask the customer to show what they've seen in another store or maybe even take a name and number to follow up with them to provide details of what they found somewhere else. There could be another product out there that your store is missing out on. Always think of the long-term relationship and how it must have a clear path for forever and a day.

This is why it's important to constantly remain at a high frequency, as you need to be that constant rock that people can fall back on. My mentor and coach, Tom Matzen, spoke on a podcast about the 100-0 rule. He explained how, before going into an interaction, you should always have the mentality and intent of giving 100% to the customer while wanting 0% in return. This, then, comes from a place of service and will ensure that customers are treated in the correct way.

I'm a huge believer in letting the work speak for itself, and this is how to gain the trust and respect of the customer by consistently doing the right thing. This is how genuine rapport is built. Always have the end goal in sight: a happy customer with a product that's right for them, not a transaction that will earn you commission or get you through your target. The more we look and listen to what the customer genuinely needs, the higher the likelihood of us showing them the right product. The more we unconditionally give, the more we receive. If there is any resistance, hesitancy, or deceit in what we're pitching or saying, there is a chance of that falsehood unraveling in the future. When it does, you're in for a world of trouble. In all probability, the customers will know that something is off anyway; there are millions of slight facial expressions and tonalities that we give off when we're being deceitful that cannot be controlled. Whether they know consciously or subconsciously that something is not right, they'll know.

For more free information about building rapport, visit https://www.fromfeartomindful.com/resources/.

Let's Take a Breather...

How's everything going? Are you getting through everything okay? Here's another tool for how to maximize your sales and be well on your way to Double Your Sales with Half the Stress In Two Years Or Less, Guaranteed. Go to a local authority or local chamber of commerce and recommend to their colleagues or members that you have a special offer just for them!

This could be a free gift, a discounted upgrade on a feature, or an included service. Never try to discount goods, as it only detracts from the value customers receive rather than building value in your company and products and services. People will jump at the chance, and whoever does come to shop in your store, you can then indoctrinate them further with another referral scheme. Genius right?!

Every year I take a select few students and help them Double Your Sales with Half the Stress In 2 Years Or Less, Guaranteed. Seventy-five percent of the fee is linked to results. Fair enough? If you'd like to apply, see if you'd be a good fit. Contact me by the means below:

info@fromfeartomindful.com

www.linkedin.com/in/sam-king-from-fear-to-mindful/

I also offer a great referral incentive to anyone who refers a salesperson or company that may benefit from this program and gets through the application process.

Spare Their Blushes

By sparing a customer's blushes, you will always maintain a deep level of rapport and have a strong chance of them buying from you. This could be when a customer makes a mistake and says something that isn't correct. In this scenario, I would say something such as, "I'm sorry I didn't explain that right; this is the specification of "Product X," or something similar. Never flat-out correct a customer, as they could easily be embarrassed and ruin their chances of purchasing. By keeping a straight face and staying neutral in the conversation, both emotionally and mentally, you let the customer gain their own composure, which is very similar to how they come to their own decision on whether the product is a good idea for them. By constantly trying to be in this state, it makes it easier as it becomes second nature.

Being Caught Off Guard

Sometimes a customer would interact with me without me instigating the conversation. Perhaps they caught me off guard when I was walking by them in the middle of a task, or perhaps collared me from behind. I never liked this, as I was caught on the back foot. As a professional salesperson however, I had to adapt my attitude, body language, and vibe, and be delicate to the conversation.

When somebody gets your attention in sales, it's human nature to instantly overreact and assume that the sale is in the bag. This categorically isn't the case, and you should always treat these scenarios the same way as you would any other sales process. Always keep your composure contained and ensure that nothing overspills. This is tricky, as you weren't expecting it, but being adaptable when life happens for you is essential to getting on. It's similar to when a girl approaches you at a bar, as long as you don't blow it and lose your composure, the chances are you'll be getting her number.

An example of this was when I had finished writing up an order for a customer and was walking to the back of the store to file the invoice. A customer asked me for help with "Product X" and wanted to know if it came in different materials. I replied that it did, and I asked them if they minded me showing them the options. They replied "no," to which I responded by showing them the fabrics and colors that were available, along with the pros and cons of them all. I then said, "Would you mind if I filed this invoice and left you to browse?" Again, they said, "No, of course not."

This helped them feel settled and respected in their original state. Their queries were answered, and they were in a safe place to discuss options. I was still in a position of authority, as my time and job seemed important and valued. I didn't put them on a pedestal by being too eager, which would have shown neediness and desperation. That, in turn, would have increased sales resistance and caused them to raise their guard, running the risk of losing the sale. There is a little bit of drama involved here, but the whole psychology of the situation worked. By delaying gratification, keeping my composure, and completing the task I set out to do while also being adaptable, I became a man of worth and respect. Everything from then on seemed to flow naturally.

Don't go off on a crusade for your own self-importance. Finding the line of serving while maintaining being an authoritative figure will increase your relationships, and ultimately sales. Once I had filed the invoice, I was on hand to proactively overcome objections and get to know their why, while answering further questions if necessary.

The Right Distance

Never be a "space invader." Allow a customer ample personal space to be comfortable while they think through their options. If they're a single person sitting at a dining table, please don't sit on the chair next to them; sit on either the left or right hand side to make sure they're comfortable and not worrying about whether you're a loony or not.

The Casual Salesperson

Nobody wants to deal with somebody they don't relate to, least of all a salesperson. This is why having a calm, relaxed, and almost casual demeanor is critical to connecting with customers and helping them buy. While this doesn't mean you're not professional in the way you communicate, you must be quite down-to-earth in your methods while having the ability to have and hold an intellectual conversation.

Whenever somebody tries to dominate, manipulate, or be aggressive in a conversation, sales resistance rises, and the chance of persuading others drops dramatically. It's almost as if you're putting on a show that the sale isn't that important to you. You must have a laissez-faire attitude; you're simply there to help them along in their journey. Of course, you want the sale, but this isn't the impression you're giving. You're neutral and detached from the sale, rather than entering into a "me vs. you" mindset.

Have you seen the meme of the dog sitting at a table in a burning room and saying, "This is fine?" Google it; it's funny, but it's relevant. Looking after yourself emotionally is crucial for this, as your EI will allow you to connect and converse with all manner of different people and personalities. Don't feel the need to be pent-up or force out your words in an aggressive manner, regardless of the stressors that are happening around you. Use the tips in "Setting the Stage: The Extra Chapter" to help present yourself in this way on a shop floor.

A customer may have asked me, "Can we get this delivered within 8 weeks?" The answer I would give was, "Maybe. Would you mind if I just go check for you?" I would respond in a casual but curious manner. Definitely not, "Yes! Absolutely we can, ma' dam!" Notice how I say "maybe"? "Maybe" is an ambiguous and neutral term that helps build more attachment between the product and the customer. It has a sense of availability and mystique about it. It also helps me stay away from the sale rather than come across as desperate or needy. It's almost keeping the sale at arm's length. Very often, I would say "maybe," even if I categorically knew the answer, to create the mindset for the reasons stated.

If anybody tells you that you should know the delivery dates of products, suggest that they change all the time. They do, although nobody has ever questioned this. When asked direct questions similar to these, always try to give answers like these, as you stay managing the sale without raising resistance. When you can't give an answer that's deflective because you'll jeopardize your position of authority or look ridiculous, drag out the agreement rather than being short, snappy, and assertive.

You can also use words like "possibly," "perhaps," "potentially," and "maybe," to downplay interactions. That helps you remain neutral from the sale, while building the need. The more we build up the product and its value, the more likely the customer is to close themselves, rather than us having to ask. Keeping your composure and status as the authority figure is critical when a customer is showing signals like this. Never get too emotional or lose your enthusiasm, just because somebody has said something that insinuates they may be buying.

Try to detach from the product or service rather than speak directly on how it'll impact the customer when describing it at first. This leaves a trail of breadcrumbs for them to pick up and it's a more classy and intelligent way of selling, rather than hammering home your point with a box ticking exercise. If a customer mentions how they have a dog, explain how a certain product is great for pets. Plant that seed to show how it will benefit them.

There are times, however, when a customer will not acknowledge what's being said, and in these cases, you need to be more direct with your approach. Maybe even challenge the customer's thought process. Being casual while still having the ability to be frank and succinct with your thoughts is essential to moving the sale along. Also, this takes a lot of emotional intelligence but can be mastered once you learn how to respond instead of reacting. Jay Abraham is an absolute genius at this; look how unflustered he is talking on stage. Take note of how he is composed and gives the impression of a cool, calm, and collected man, but his mind is as sharp as ever and ready to pounce.

For more free information on how to detach yourself from the sale, visit https://www.fromfeartomindful.com/resources/.

Chapter 6

Knowing how to serve customers correctly is so important to lowering sales resistance and keeping relationships strong. The next few pages will tell you exactly how to do that in a subtle manner while keeping you in a position of authority.

Asking the Right Questions in the Right Manner

As we know, customers walking into a store are most likely a little defensive and apprehensive. It's our job as sales professionals to disarm this negativity from the get-go. The way we do this is by asking questions that will get the response we want while leaving the customer in the same state they were originally in. What word are people drawn to use when asked a question when they're feeling defensive? "No."

This is why, as salespeople, we must help enable the customer to use this response when asking them a question while still getting the positive answer that we need to progress the sale. Sounds tricky, right? Not really. By simply changing the way that questions are asked, we can take away the sales resistance and get customers to come around to our way of thinking even quicker while dropping their guard.

Try asking questions such as, "Would you be opposed to me showing you products that might be suitable?"

"Would you mind if I checked the delivery time of this product?"

You could also try something like, "Would you be against the idea of…"

It is extremely unlikely that a customer will respond to these questions with, "Yes, I would mind if you showed me some products that were available."

There is a chance that this could happen, and when it does, simply step away from the interaction and let your customer look at it in their own time, being sensitive to their position. This way you can manage and influence the sale while leaving the customer feeling comfortable. They'll think they're the ones who are leading the sale, even though they may be a little bewildered! A perfect example of this was when a customer came in and showed me a picture of a sofa from a competitor that was extremely similar to the one we had.

I greeted them like usual. "Hi guys, are you just looking or are you looking for something in particular?"

Customer: "We've actually seen this sofa we like at Store X and wondered if you had anything similar?"

I take a look at the picture and get a little excited because I know just the one they'll be having, but I have to maintain my demeanor of being cool, calm, and collected.

Me: "Would you mind if I showed you a similar product and then just leave you to browse?

"Customer: "No. Go ahead." The customer sees the sofas.

Customer: "Oh, ok."

Still stay calm and keep the enthusiasm bubbling away.

Me: "Would you mind if I showed you the samples and colors that it's available in and then just leave you to browse?"

"No," they answered.

I knew they were buying it from the moment I saw the picture, as the product was of higher quality and the deal was luckily better as we had a promotion, but I still had to play the game and let them be the ones who made their own mind up. I couldn't assume anything that could compromise the sale. This was laying everything out for the customer to make an informed decision for themselves while I still led the sale.

When asking these questions, you should ask them either at the start of the interaction or at least in the early stages. Until rapport is built, you should ask the questions in a tone of slight uncertainty. The uncertainty portrays that you're a little unsure whether you can help the customer out or not, but you're going to see what you can do. An example could be: "Would you mind…if I showed you a few similar products… and then just leave you to browse?" Remember to pause to help draw the customer into what you're saying, and use body language and facial expression to insinuate the slight uncertainty. Even if a customer was on a product and I knew from the buying signals they were almost certainly going to buy it, I would still open the conversation with the same phrase. It kept the resistance down and made me appear as a helpful salesperson rather than one who was only in it for the commission.

Always keep up this questioning technique through the entire process, even if the customer has already bought. It'll maintain the energy and create a seamless experience for the customer while keeping you at the right frequency for the day ahead. Sometimes I've gotten too excited at the point of writing up an order and forgotten this technique, only to lose the flow of momentum. This is hard work, but staying our best professional selves keeps the sales relationship open for more purchases, as it keeps you in a deep level of rapport.

For an extra free resource about this topic, visit https://www.fromfeartomindful.com/resources/.

Never Allow Somebody To Buy The First Product They See... Just Yet

How many times have you spoken with a customer who has fallen in love with the first item they laid eyes on? Numerous, I'm guessing. Whenever I would serve somebody who did this, of course I would add value and proactively overcome objections by giving information about the product, but I would insist quite early in the interaction: "Don't buy the first one you see; there are plenty more to look at!"

This would be said as a joke, and the majority of times, I'd get a laugh and an agreement. However, there was meaning behind this. This attitude helps you build credibility by showing you care about the customers' choices and are not just interested in the sale. It's also looking out for the customers' best interests. We both know that they'll more than likely go back to the original one, but that's not the point! Customers need to feel as if they've shopped around and come to the right decision. It also adds to the entire experience of being out shopping in a wonderful store.

Even if they were dead set on a certain product, I would challenge them to have a further look around the store just to ensure they were making the right choice; it was my moral obligation. Obviously, if a customer was certain and dead set on not looking around, I wouldn't cause a scene, but you get where I'm coming from.

For more free resources on how to implement this as well as others, visit https://www.fromfeartomindful.com/resources/.

Find Out Their "Why"

Many salespeople only look at the surface level of what a customer wants, when really, they need to get why they want or need it. They might just say they're looking for a new product, but why are they looking for a new product? Try to delve deep into their motives to give yourself and them a better idea of why they're with you. Ask questions such as these to delve a little deeper into their position: "What have you got at the moment? How long have you had it? Are you looking for something similar? Why are you replacing it?" What situation are they in that's enabled them to decide they need something new? Perhaps this has an effect on their choice. Is it because they've moved houses? Has the old one seen better days? If so, why is it worn? Have they got a family, children, or pets? Have they redecorated? All these scenarios will help the customer reveal their true intentions. This then gives us a better platform to provide them with the best service possible and find them the perfect product choice.

All of this helps affirm to the customer that they do need a new product because of the situation that they've just verbalized. However, this can't be the intention, as it could be considered sly and manipulative. The reason we must get their why is to provide the best service. At the same time, we're acting as sponges and taking in all the relevant information that will help us potentially sell more products. If they've moved houses, do they need other products to fill the property? If their old product is worn out but only due to heavy impact from children and pets, perhaps a better-quality product or a higher-grade option? Thicker leather, more durable fabrics, etc. If they've redecorated, what other products could they need? Maybe they need accessories to change the entire face of the room instead of just swapping a product out for something similar. Never say, "Oh, you'll be needing a new product X because of situation Y," whenever a customer lets slip a piece of information that you use to help further purchases. Instead, keep it under your figurative hat and bring this information out once they confirm they're buying a product. If a customer mentions that they need other items, acknowledge this, but then say something along the lines of, "Ok, great, would you mind if we get this sorted first before we start looking at other items?" Your customer will appreciate this, as it allows them to focus on the matter at hand rather than thinking of too many options. You've also just said to them how they'll get this sorted first, or however you'd like to phrase it, which has insinuated they'll be making a decision on this subject before proceeding to look at something else, i.e. they're making a decision and buying a product before moving on. Salespeople should spend more time finding out about the customers' "why" and how the product will suit them rather than pitching and presenting the product. If this isn't the case, the salesperson is selling rather than consulting.

Imagine you're at the doctor's office. Does the doctor simply look at your ailment and decide how and why a certain product is the right one for you? Of course not. They ask a series of questions and perhaps ask for a second opinion to confirm the right course of action to take. If they don't, the results could be disastrous.

Sales isn't life or death, but not hitting your target is pretty disastrous too. So, try to act as a consultant and really hone in on their needs with intent, then act based on your experiences.

Keep Adding Value, Even When A Customer is Dismissive

When a customer walks around and settles on a product, provide valuable information about it, regardless of how they spoke with you coming into the store. They might have been abrupt or dismissive of you, but create a connection between yourself and the customer, whilst also giving the impression that you're being helpful rather than sales-y. It's also a fantastic opportunity to proactively overcome potential objections that may occur during the presentation. I've seen salespeople who have had their head chewed off by customers as they walked in during the meet and greet. They then lose their confidence and avoid serving them. Build the resilience to be in a mentality that you're there to serve, irrelevant to what the customer's attitude is. Perhaps they're just having a bad day, perhaps they're sick of salespeople as they may have been speaking to them all day long, who knows. As long as you're genuinely adding value and doing your job, nobody can bring you down for it.

Deliver this information assertively and confidently while staying out of an aggressive tone. Use phrases such as 'You can get this in (insert your product options here)'

Having and maintaining the confidence even when a customer has been dismissive is imperative to build a connection and rapport. Even customers who have been frosty during the meet and greet should be spoken to in this manner. However, it is great practice to hold your hands up in a way of saying "I'm not forcing a sale here, I'm simply doing my job and I'm here to help if you need it" when you give them space to look. This diffuses tension, lowers sales resistance and leaves you as the advisor they need rather than the salesperson they don't want.

Resist trying to smash through sales barriers. Helping customers unconditionally causes them to lower their guard in their own time making the interaction more relaxed and resistance free. Once you've added value to prove to them you may be worthy of their time, ask about their why. It would take a really hardened customer to not acknowledge your curiosity when you've shown willingness first. They're out there but keep going. I'd loved the challenge of this kind of customer and I kept going until they'd finally relent and tell me their needs. I saw it almost as a battle of wills and who would give in first. Obviously, this was carried out in a classy, service driven manner, but I'd always take on the challenge and rise to the occasion. People are in the store for a reason. The difference between a good salesperson and a great salesperson is that great salespeople are positive and take on the challenge, rather than backing down. Love the grind of serving when nothing seems to be going your way. When you start to embrace the hard times as opportunities to grow, you're on the right path to be the top of your game.

For more information on how to stay positive, visit https://www.fromfeartomindful.com/resources/.

Unconditional Giving

Whenever I used to serve customers who were a little bit icy in their demeanor or perhaps just a tad unsure, I would always write down or circle details of the products they were looking at on the specification cards and hand them over without the need to be prompted. This would give the impression that I was genuinely looking after their best interests, and it had a hint of reverse psychology to its methods. People would ask me to write things down, so by already doing it, I disarmed them of the objection. I'd note down the sizes and other things to make it easier for customers to measure at home and emit a vibe of service. I used to circle sizes all the time because, when selling furniture, one of the biggest objections is knowing whether the product will fit or not. By helping them in this but leaving the customer to make their own mind up, I spurred them on to lower their guard. That helped me gain a little influence over their decision-making since they started to trust me. I wasn't giving it to them and forgetting about them; it was something I did in order for them to feel valued and become accustomed to my presence. If they were still looking at a particular product, I would then proceed to add more value or ask questions about their why. This method helped me gain likability and credibility.

Never Take Anything For Granted

If a customer comes into the store to see a specific item, then the chances are quite high that they'll buy it. I'd still run through the process of showing more options to affirm that this one is the one they're buying, as nothing should be taken for granted, especially in sales. If a customer was virtually decided on a product, I'd still keep my composure and ask them, "Sure, would you mind if I show you and then leave you to browse?" The answer will almost certainly be no, which, as we've discussed before, is the perfect answer to leave customers in the state they're in. It also insinuates that you aren't taking it as gospel that the customer is buying; you're simply allowing them the time and space to look in their own time. The second you let your emotions run away with you, the chances of losing the sale increase, so make sure to keep your composure and enthusiasm bubbling away. Then follow the steps in this book to close the deal seamlessly. Even though this particular customer has come in to look at a certain product, I would still recommend that they look around to see if other models could be a good fit. I'd even suggest a few that I thought could work. This wasn't to put the customer off, but it's an example of me kicking the can down the road and not giving the impression that I wasn't desperate for the sale. It also made the customer feel valued and even more reassured. I was showing them more options to choose from and ensuring that they were making the right choice. People love the idea of shopping around, as it makes them feel as if they're making the correct choice. I'd show them as many as I could without being unreasonable or over the top to try and exhaust their need for looking around. If they were happy with the choices in store, then there was less likelihood that they would feel the need to look elsewhere. Even if they did look at the competition, at least I had given them great service and left them in a better place than I had found them. Plus, I left a great impression of myself and the company I worked for.

Acknowledge the Objection

In any scenario, always acknowledge any objection that a customer may have. Never overlook it or just bypass it, as the customer will feel mistreated and undervalued. Use phrases such as:

"I feel...what you went through..."

"I get...you need it within 8 weeks..."

Then follow these up with how you'll overcome them, such as:

"...but we're a different business who prides ourselves on..." "...but wouldn't it be worth waiting an extra 2 weeks to have the product you really want?"

Simply by acknowledging how the customer feels and what they're going through, you're disarming them from potential future disagreements. The majority will give you a chance to prove yourself. Sure, there are some customers that won't relent, but all you can do is do your best and leave the decision up to them in a caring, sensitive manner. Never ignore a question, especially one on price. I've been on a sales call where I've asked the price of something, only for the salesman to completely ignore what I'm asking and carry on with their pitch regardless. It was very rude and hinted that whatever the price was, it wasn't worth it. Always answer a question immediately when it's asked to create more credibility, trust, and transparency. People can tell when you're being sleazy, manipulative, or telling half-truths from the subliminal changes in your tonality and body language. Maybe you become aggressive, awkward, or embarrassed. Save everyone's blushes by not engaging in these behaviors and treating your customers the way they deserve to be treated.

Know When to be the Leading Actor Or Play the Supporting Role

I would never try to be the center of attention, but when I had to step into the shoes of the leading figure, I gladly made the choice and played it well. For example, I would describe features, benefits, or specifications about a product to a customer. Since I was the authority figure, I had to know what I was talking about and clearly articulate it. Sounds pretty obvious, right?

The issue some salespeople have is knowing when it's their time to step out of the spotlight and let the customers take the lead. When it's time for the customer to answer or think about options, we have to be focused on that rather than jostling for position. If this isn't applied correctly, salespeople can easily be perceived as arrogant or rude. Examples of these are:

- Talking over customers.
- Having to have the final word.
- Not actively listening.

- Not applying full focus to the interaction, i.e., looking around the room, tapping your fingers.

- Letting your emotions overspill, resulting in customers feeling rushed or turned off.

I know these are simple social awareness skills, but they play a huge part in creating and strengthening relationships that last forever. The higher your emotional awareness and resilience, the higher your chances of building that rapport and relationship, regardless of the customer's attitude or mindset. Metaphorically, stepping out of the spotlight gives them space to think, digest, or converse about what we've discussed or what I've shown. This could be when customers were looking at something for themselves, whether it be colors or fabrics, or perhaps discussing options with their other half. I had to very quickly learn how to turn off the need to be the center of attention and then let the attention be on the subject at hand. Whether that be the color choice, specification options, working out sizes, etc.

Then, I'd detach myself from the conversation, letting the information be digested. As I keep saying, letting customers make up their own minds in their own time and not trying to be in control of every little detail of the process works wonders. People can't feel hurried into making a decision, as their guard instantly rises. It is a longer way of selling, but it's the most effective. Instead of thinking small and being in control of every little part of the interaction, try to think of the process as one big interaction. Your end game is them writing up the order, and possibly future orders, rather than debating potential objections that lead up to that point. Even if that order may take a few extra visits or phone calls.

I'd learn how to shut down the need to be center stage and allow my customers to play their part while still being on hand if any queries needed to be answered. I also kept my gravitas and enthusiasm bubbling away. Imagine you're boiling some potatoes; there's too much heat, and the water is spilling over, creating a mess and wreaking havoc in the process. Too little heat, and the potatoes will take ages to cook, if at all! This is why finding the sweet spot and sticking to it is the perfect way to provide efficient service. By finding this point, you'll have more influence over the sale. You'll also have the ability to serve other customers at the same time because your time value has increased. Never take on too much, or you'll run the risk of your saucepan overflowing and losing the results that you've worked hard for. This could mean doing things like:

- Not answering the phone when in discussions with a customer

- Not serving too many customers to keep your focus at optimal efficiency

- Completing a task before entering into a new one

- Prioritizing tasks rather than dealing with them as they come

Just like with your emotional battery, you only have a finite level of focus. Spread it too thin, and it won't be enough to sustain the tasks and complete them effectively.

I remember one particular day when everything was going right for me. Every customer I touched was booking, but the thing was, they were huge orders. By the fifth or sixth order, I was starting to feel overwhelmed. In all honesty, the pressure was getting to be a bit much. My then sales manager mentioned how I needed to prioritize which orders I had to deal with first before moving on to the next ones.

Was one already in the bag but just needed a phone call to confirm?

Was it just a case of choosing a certain option but being happy to take their time?

Was one desperate for advice and running the risk of walking if I wasn't on hand to answer?

By taking a second to compose myself, take stock of the situation, and ask these questions, I was able to make a plan of attack for how I would tackle each situation. As it turned out, every order went fine, but it was only because I composed myself and addressed them with a clear mind. The higher your level of focus, the more you'll be able to deal with. This is why looking after yourself emotionally by not entering into self-sabotaging behaviors, situations, and conversations that don't serve you is critical to succeeding.

I heard a story of a term that the Special Air Service (SAS) uses called the "Grey Man," which I find fascinating. They mentioned that to survive under interrogation or in hostage scenarios, a person must be present and yet, not fully present. They must act in such a way that they're almost a fly on the wall, taking everything in but giving very little back. When they do decide to drip-feed information, it's extremely concise and on point, but it doesn't compromise their position of authority or worth. They may give the impression of a disheveled, inoffensive, and harmless person. In reality, they're simply containing their innermost emotions and trying to keep the spotlight away from them by putting it on another subject.

While you should never be evasive or completely ambiguous with your customers, knowing when to drip-feed information at the right time is critical to remaining a credible person who is worthy of their respect. Avoid having a meltdown and letting all the information out at once. This also builds value in the product and only strengthens its attachment to the end user.

Ever heard the expression, "Slowly, slowly, catch a monkey?" I remember I was out shopping once and overheard a customer asking a specific detail about a mattress, for the salesperson to answer and then go on to describe how the drawers on the divan were great quality. It was just a comical exchange where the salesperson didn't plan out methodically what the customer was looking for, and that resulted in a confused potential purchaser. Instead of asking why, they were asking for a specific detail. This really is a simple social skill that can be used in any interaction. Of course, you have an agenda; you're a salesperson, but all you're doing is providing great service.

As you're talking with a person or people that are on the same social hierarchy as you, never talk down to anybody and never talk up to anybody. This will only make it harder to talk openly about subjects that need to be addressed, and you're opening yourself up for the customer to become disagreeable about what's being said. When you're talking with somebody as though they're an esteemed colleague, you're able to have a much more open conversation about a subject that could be classified as touchy with somebody else. They're also more likely to simply accept what you're saying and move on from the topic. This is the ideal relationship to have with customers.

Don't Create Jealousy

Whenever I was serving a couple, I would always try to sit or stand next to the man. rather than the woman, to stop any jealousy arising within the couple. Before you say how big-headed I am, think about it. It's a natural reaction for many people to experience jealousy when their spouse is talking to another person, especially when they're a young, good-looking salesman like me. I did this purely for the fact that I wanted to lower resistance for all parties and so that we were all on the same frequency, creating pure transparency. Please bear in mind that the majority of the time, it's the woman who will make the final decision. This may offend people, especially in this day and age, but it's true.

Always make sure all parties' opinions are heard and valued too. It's almost as if you're acting as a mediator between everybody while providing facts in order for them to make an informed choice for themselves.

Compose Yourself Before Giving an Answer or Any Interaction

In the book *Think & Grow Rich*, there is a paragraph that talks about one of America's most successful and best financiers and how he would close his eyes before making a decision. When I was asked a question, I would pause to compose myself before giving an answer too. This allowed me to take stock of the question that was being asked and ensure that my mind was in the right place to give a correct answer without compromising my position.

Very often, when under pressure, people can ask you questions you aren't prepared for. If you're not careful, you can fall into the trap of giving flippant or hot-headed answers that will have a detrimental effect on your future and success. Be mindful and remove the knot from within your stomach to be freer with your thoughts, movement, and speech. It's not very often that I would close my eyes, but I would get my mind in the right place to make a clear and concise decision that would benefit all parties, including my own. It also allowed me to remain in the authority position because I took a moment to consider the options while creating gravitas. This is what leaders do: they weigh up both sides of the equation and come to a relevant answer. Even before answering the store phone, I would stop for a second to compose myself before I answered it. Sure, it could just have been somebody checking the status of the order, but it could also have been a customer wanting to place an order too. Irrelevant to who it is, always compose yourself before the interaction to give yourself the best possible chance of receiving a positive result.

Customers deserve that level of focus and attention. We've all been there, serving a customer and writing up a deal that was great. We all felt that rush of adrenaline. However, you can't just dive into the next customer, as they won't be on the same level of energy as you. How could they be? You and your previous customer have just come to an agreement, and all parties are high-energy since everybody is happy. If you then go to serve somebody who is in a just-looking state with the same energy, their sales resistance will be high, and instantly you'll repel them. Always take the time to center yourself before interacting with other prospective customers.

The same goes for when you've had a negative interaction with somebody. Under no circumstances should you ever take your frustration out on another customer simply because something has annoyed you. Sure, the interaction may not have been your fault; it could have been because of an unruly customer or colleague. Perhaps you're just having a bad day, but one thing is for certain: it definitely isn't the customer's fault. If you're not in a 100% centered state, then don't interact with anybody. You won't have the focus to provide great service and almost certainly won't have the gravitas to be able to influence others.

This practice wasn't always the case for me. I used to enter frequencies that didn't serve me, i.e., rushing to beat other sales-people to a customer, losing my head, diving straight into another potential sale, etc. Over time, I learned that this wasn't what the customer needed from a salesperson. When I realized this wasn't the case and accepted that it was me that needed to be centered and have 100% certainty in myself to be successful, I stopped rushing to customers and letting my emotions get the better of me. Many times, I would let other salespeople rush. Sometimes the customers bought with them, sometimes they didn't. It was irrelevant because I knew that by concentrating on myself and keeping my state of focus, at some point I would be at the top, but only as long as I kept my focus indefinitely. Some people use swinging techniques, where they swing their arms or handbags to ground themselves into a centered state. I've known some people who even sway their bodies. Personally, I concentrate on my breathing to calm my emotions down enough to provide a sense of calm and solidity within my body, along with the techniques I've described before.

Don't think of what could have been or what will happen in the future; this is where depression and anxiety form. Instead, concentrate on the here and now and how you can do the best job possible. As I've mentioned, people love to be served by people they can relate to and are a pleasure to be around, so be that cool, calm, and collected person.

A Stoic Mindset

Having an unshakable mindset is so important to remain in the same state of flow. I could talk for hours about the importance of having a stoic mindset, but this parable about an old Chinese farmer that Alan Watts retold describes it perfectly:

Once upon a time, there was a Chinese farmer whose horse ran away. That evening, all his neighbors came around to commiserate. They said, "We are so sorry to hear your horse has run away. This is most unfortunate." The farmer said, "Maybe." The next day the horse came back, bringing seven wild horses with it, and in the evening, everybody came back and said, "Oh, isn't that lucky? What a great turn of events! You now have eight horses!" The farmer again said, "Maybe."

The following day, his son tried to break one of the horses, and while riding it, he was thrown and broke his leg. The neighbors then said, "Oh dear, that's too bad," and the farmer responded, "Maybe." The next day, the conscription officers came around to conscript people into the army, and they rejected his son because he had a broken leg. Again, all the neighbors came around and said, "Isn't that great!?" Again, he said, "Maybe."

> *"The whole process of nature is an integrated process of immense complexity, and it's really impossible to tell whether anything that happens is good or bad—because you never know what will be the consequence of the misfortune; or, you never know what will be the consequence of good fortune." - Alan Watts.*

The more you can stop negative energies from entering your world and almost detach yourself from the situation, the more successful you'll be. Yes, there is a sense of ambiguity here, but as long as it doesn't verge on manipulation and you're transparent when you have to be, that's sales.

Ever the Optimist

We can't just decide to flick a switch and change our state, as it's too much hard work. As we've discussed, people like constants. Therefore, we need to be in that state of absolute certainty, positivity, and enthusiasm at all times.

When the store isn't busy, we still need to be in that state. We can't just turn it on as the customer comes around the corner and enters the store; we already should be living it. On a busy Saturday, wherever I worked, I would always remind myself to be in that state of certainty, confidence, and positivity by envisioning where the next customer would come from when things started to get a little bit tense.

I'd clear my mind and expect customers to walk through the door. I had to be ready for the event to take place. I felt that customers had a sixth sense, and if I wasn't at my absolute best, they would sense it, and I'd run the risk of losing a possible sale. I'd take it to another level by imagining the next customer I'd be serving driving into the parking lot. It even got to a stage where I'd imagine them leaving their house and making their way in to make a purchase! It's funny looking back now, but that's how serious I was about making sure I was on point and ready for them. It was a way of almost manifesting the customers that I was going to serve. Maybe that's true, maybe it isn't, but it did make me become my best self to serve the next customer that walked through the door, and that's what counts.

When working with colleagues, you still must be the most on-point person. Shop floors are like the jungle. As soon as you let your guard down, other salespeople will sniff this out, and you'll lose your place in the pecking order. Please don't look at this as a negative; it's a fantastic way of making sure you're in your best form at all times. Remember, iron sharpens iron, and we need to excel in every challenge that is thrown at us. Never back down, and always take on the challenge. When I was at my peak, I only got there because I was working with the sharpest of salespeople. This made me work harder, as I had to step up and raise my game in order to beat them. Sure, there were some underhanded behaviors, but that's not the point. It's to be expected wherever you work in sales. I had to raise my level in order to win, and by accepting what was happening, surrendering, and adapting to it, I gained momentum and shone.

If you keep persisting and staying positive, you'll be number one too. Throughout the week, I'd be calling leads and speaking to people who I'd spoken to prior, trying to drum up business to keep the flow of energy flowing. This compounding effort kept stacking up, and eventually it paid dividends. Very often, a customer would come in or call out of the blue, ready to place an order because of the work I had put in prior. To an outsider, it would look as if I was lucky, but they were only seeing the end result; they weren't aware of the work I had put in to get to this point.

Let Attachment Build Before Presenting

Never rush over to a customer just because somebody has stopped at a product and is showing an interest in it. Let them experience the product first. Let them feel what it's all about and take it in its entirety. They're also taking in their surroundings, including you, especially at the start of the process. Being emotionally aware and keeping your composure man-aged is essential to gain the trust of the customer.

I read one article that said you should only start your full presentation if you believe there is a 50% or greater chance that they'll buy. While I think there is partial truth to this, I'm not too sure, as it's based on how the salesperson perceives the customer. Are you a "glass half full" or "glass half empty" kind of person?

I would speak to customers that other salespeople had no intention of serving because they "weren't buying," only for me to be shaking their hand, leaving them carrying an in-voice and a smile on their face only a few minutes later. The fact is people come into a store for a reason. Of course, there is a chance of them buying, no matter how small. I believe in the subtler side of our approach: using the right body language, questioning methods, and being in the right frequencies. The more we do that, the more likely the "lesser percentages" are to going buy. Don't judge them on their body language or stereotypical buying signals. If they're still looking at a product, that's one of the biggest buying signals you can have! I remember serving an old lady who everybody thought was a waste of time. I slowed my body and frequency down to match hers, so we connected.

I said, "Hi, are you just looking or are you looking for something in particular?"

To which she gave me her answers, and then I gave her fantastic service at the speed that was appropriate to her and ended the presentation, leaving all options on the table for her to choose from. When I say, "all options," it was only down to color choice, as she had everything else figured out. She simply said, "I think I'm going to go for that one."

"Are you sure?" I asked.

"Yes, quite sure." Boom. The lady didn't need a stereotypically assertive or direct salesperson losing their composure and being in her space. She needed somebody who was on her level to let her make her own mind up while she came to an informed decision. This was the perfect example of how making the interaction about the customer rather than our own ego is crucial to winning.

The same goes when you come across a customer who is direct and wants to manage of the sale, let them, and remember to keep up with their energy. Don't feel the need to bring their energy down. As long as you keep your enthusiasm contained and remember the same questioning techniques: uncovering their why and giving them enough emotional space to take in all the options, you'll gain their respect and start to manage the sale. This kind of behavior: being agreeable and acting almost chameleon-like, will allow you to get along with most people. Plus, you'll still allow the energy and momentum to flow, creating more sales orders. The more able you're available to connect with other people's frequency with empathy, the more you'll be able to sell.

Some customers demand a deep level of effort from you, but you've got to be willing to go to that place in order to get what you want: an order. If you aren't willing to put in the work, then you aren't worthy of their money. This may sound harsh, but it's true. Embrace the hard times, as not everything will always go your way. Try to treat these as tests. There comes a stage in every sales process with a customer where you need to surrender to the interaction. Like Shiraz said before, "You must be willing to have your heart broken in order to have a fulfilling relationship." It's the exact same here. If you aren't willing to be vulnerable for the short-term, you'll never achieve your potential. If you're worthy of enduring the stress and are still providing great service, then the universe will have a way of paying it back. Either with this customer or the next, provided you stay strong and keep going.

Ever heard the expression, "The harder you work, the luckier you get?" Even if the customer doesn't buy, you'll have had vital experience that you'll be able to learn from for next time. Whether that be the mannerisms of a certain customer type or how deep you should go next time in order to succeed, you're learning. Never leave anything on the line and have regrets or what-ifs. If something needs to be said, say it. Never feel anxious or worried about the consequences or what other people might think. If what you have to say adds value, it's your moral obligation to provide that.

The consequence could be an awkward exchange with your sales manager when you have to justify why you haven't hit your target. The same goes for spending time with people who don't make a purchase. Through your experience, you'll learn more quickly to weed out the ones who are and aren't ready to purchase. However, you must be willing to take the risk of giving them your full attention and seeing it through all of the way. This is the only way you'll learn.

When you've surrendered to the situation and are proceeding to give a full presentation, don't give all the information at once. Drip-feeding instead is the best option. Provide no more than three pieces of information at any one time. If they're interested, they'll spend more time on a product than somebody who isn't. If they're taking notes, collecting information, or looking through different options, they're interested. This is a perfect time to engage and proactively overcome objections that they could be experiencing at that very moment. If they're looking at samples, mention something like, "Some samples are harder-wearing than others." Then delve into the differences and ask the customer why a certain benefit would be better than others depending on their product choice.

Do they have pets? Do they have children? All of these questions build up the picture of the perfect product while cementing your position as a caring, trustworthy salesperson. Perhaps there is a price difference too, which you could explain and the reasons why. Whenever you do this, offer another piece of information from your checklist that will add value to the customer's experience and decision. They probably weren't even aware of these factors. Once you've given the information, simply hand them a specification card with the details on it, if one's available. This shows that you're helping them with their experience rather than selling, which lowers sales resistance and builds trust. It should never get to the stage where a customer is defensive or says that they're just looking. If it does, that means that you've said something that has triggered their resistance and caused them to raise their guard. I used to be quite quick when handing over cards once I gave information so as to acknowledge their just-looking state before they mentioned it. The second somebody says something defensive like this, the chances are the sale will be lost since it's difficult to get them to lower their guard again.

Leaving Customers to Stew

We all know the best stews or curries are the ones that are left alone to sit in their own juices. The same goes when people are purchasing. Providing time and space for customers to think is essential for them to come to an informed decision by themselves, especially if they're wary of their surroundings. You must still be close enough to answer any questions that need to be answered while giving them enough distance to think. Fred Sirieix from *First Dates*, a TV show in the UK, explained it perfectly. A waiter should be almost like a ghost; they should appear exactly when they need to and then disappear in an instant, almost like magic. This approach is the perfect analogy for sales.

Don't take this as an excuse to go gossiping by the water fountain or standing on your phone; you need to remain at the same frequency and have the same energy to maintain the level of rapport and focus. Momentum is your best friend, so try to make sure nothing hinders it. Just because you're not actively engaging doesn't mean you're not working or building rapport. This also helps you serve other customers at the same time, as you're able to free up your time. This should be explained to the customers that you're serving too, as this will keep them in the loop and informed at all stages of the process. This transparency only helps build trust.

Keeping customers in the loop and informed is so important, whether that be serving somebody else, taking a phone call, or simply letting them know you're leaving them to browse. When I left customers to their own devices, I would still be thinking of ideas that would be suitable for their needs. I'd think of what would be good, and if I thought of one, I'd voice the suggestion. If I couldn't think of any, I'd let them know that too, as it showed I was giving them my full attention and acting with intent.

Observe Rather Than Getting Involved

When you come from a place of observation, you've mentally detached yourself from the scenario that is taking place. This technique is a must for any top salesperson.

Just because you're observing doesn't mean you're not still focused. You must be fully attentive at all times, even if you look chilled. Imagine being a TV on standby. The power is still running through, but nothing is being shown.

Have you seen Rocky IV, where Steps mentions that the dog isn't doing much because he's "dead"? Rocky, on the other hand, knows that "Punchy" isn't "wasting his energy." This is another example of containing your enthusiasm.

See and acknowledge what is unfolding in front of you rather than being at the epicenter. When you are the outsider looking in, you get a much more detailed and neutral story. Plus, it allows you to manage the sale much better.

This method also gives your customers and clients the physical and emotional space they need to make a decision while lowering sales resistance. This is where you become more of an "advisor" than a "salesperson." Whenever you come from a consultative point of view, people will warm to you more and appreciate your authority.

Never Show Too Many Products

Never show more than two to three products to a customer who has explained to you what an ideal product would be, especially when they've just walked into the store. This will run the risk of almost certainly losing credibility as an authority figure. This can also be extremely annoying, as sometimes you can show somebody something that fits the description perfectly, only for them not to like it. However, this is personal preference and taste, and we have to adapt to that. After the third "no," simply ask the customer, "Would you mind if I leave you to browse while I check for other products that may be suitable?" This alleviates the pressure of having to pick something up there and leaves the customer to browse at their own leisure instead of being led around the store. This emotional respite will help clear the minds of both you and the customer and contribute to a seamless experience. Give the impression you're there in an advisory capacity rather than selling to add to their experience.

It also lets the customer think that you're an authority figure thinking further on their issue. Always let them know that this is what you're doing to be fully transparent and keep them in the loop. Give the idea some thought and make any suggestions that come to mind. Perhaps you need to ask further questions to get their why and what they're really looking for to get a better understanding. Check online or in any brochures that you may have and show those options too.

When presenting products, don't show them and tick off all of the points that they possess that may benefit your customer; this can be extremely tedious. Simply show the product with open arm gestures and let them decide for themselves whether it's a good fit. You'll know by their body language and instant reaction whether they like it or not. If a customer falls in love with the first product you present, remind them not to buy the first one they see and say something like, "I appreciate you like this, but would you mind if I show you some others so you have some good options to choose from? I'd rather you see everything so you make the right choice." This detaches you from the sale further and confirms you're simply advising the customer and looking after their best interests rather than selling. Note how I say, "choose from?" That insinuates that they'll be picking one of the options of the products that they're looking at today. Notice how I say, "so you make the right choice?" Again, this anchors in that they'll be making a choice with you and empowers them, regardless of what they choose. Don't force or rush them onto the next option, let the attachment build. You'll be able to absorb more information about their ideal product and place it in the experience.

Proactively Overcoming Objections

This is what real service is all about: explaining and going out of your way to find out information that will help the customer pick a product in their own time. Through your experience, you'll be able to figure out what objections people are coming up with, and you'll be able to incorporate these into your presentation. Take a sofa, for example. For a sofa, some objections could be:

Configuration	Accessibility
Size	Delivery time
Fabric options	Price
Color	Ethical matters
Leather thickness	Time constraint
Recliner options	

Can you think of any more basic objections? Can you think of basic objections that are relevant to your industry?

Create a checklist of them in your mind and make sure that they've all been checked off before closing the deal. Don't close unless they've all been discussed. This ensures that you and the customer know that the product is right for them, and again, they realize that you care about their choice rather than just talking with them for the commission. You may think these objections seem trivial but look into the customers' eyes. Every detail is new to them, and therefore it's our responsibility to make them aware of all the aspects of the sale before they purchase, gaining credibility in the process.

I really used to enjoy this method, as it was quite analytical. Some objections may come up at different parts of the sales process, and that's fine; we must be flexible enough to cope with this. If another objection comes up that the majority of people will find beneficial, then incorporate that into your future pitches to take the pressure off the customer.

Don't worry or get flustered by objections. Objections are fantastic, as they mean one thing: the customer is interested. Keeping your cool and thinking logically rather than emotionally when objections are thrown at you is essential to overcoming them. The second you react emotionally, you're losing your influence over the sale.

I always tried to bring up the objections before the customer mentioned them, as it alleviated the pressure from them and made me look like a professional. I used to hate it when a customer brought up an objection that I hadn't mentioned that was on my list as it loosened my grip, and I lost influence. Although, I would obviously never be offended or take my frustration out on them. If you've delved into the whys of the customer well enough, there should be no objections. Objections only occur when you haven't covered a subject that the customer wishes to hear.

Demonstrating the Benefits of the Features

Demonstrating the benefit of a feature rather than describing it is a much more tactile way of selling that creates a little drama and involves the customer in the process. They also get real-life experience of how the products work. For example, instead of describing how a table extends, just show it. Ask if they have a big family or if they have people around for dinner parties while demonstrating the benefits of the features. This gets the customer to grow an attachment to the product as they visualize and hear about its uses.

When sofas come with a recliner option, show them the smooth mechanism instead of telling them. I made the mistake of engaging the recliner of a seat when a customer was sitting on it once, and even though they didn't say anything, they weren't impressed. I put this down to my eagerness and never did it again. Demonstrate a seat that's not being used or the one you're sitting in. Describe to the customer where they can find their control so they can do it for themselves; this helps them grow even more attachment to the product.

Even if a benefit of the product wouldn't be of any use to the customer, explain and show it anyway, along with the rest. It'll only increase the value of the product and tempt the customer over the edge into purchasing it. I've heard of a store that sells kitchens in the USA that lets their customers cook and prepare meals, and their sales have skyrocketed. Can anybody be surprised? By involving customers emotionally, they're much more likely to buy. How can you get a customer emotionally involved in your sales process with a product you sell?

Don't Overload with Information

Research shows giving a customer three or more pieces of information in a single interaction is detrimental to the sale as it can mentally overload them. I can confirm this to be the case through my own experiences. By dripping out information in stages, we slowly allow the customer to ease their way into the product that they're starting to love and grow an emotional attachment to.

Knowing When to Go Back In

The timing of any interaction has got to be correct, but be aware that there is no perfect time to speak with a customer. Sometimes life happens, and you just have to bite the bullet and go for it. However, under no circumstances should you rush in, act out, or worse, take your frustration out on the customer just because they aren't at a frequency that serves you. It's their purchase and their experience, and we must adjust to that as professionals. Work a little harder to ensure the customers relate to you by collecting your thoughts and centering yourself. Use the techniques we've discussed. This will give you the confidence to help in the way they deserve and will achieve the best results.

People often tell me that they feel unsure or awkward about interacting with customers, and they don't know when the best time to do it is. The issue isn't that there is a perfect time; it's the fact that most people feel anxious and awkward and build these make-believe walls between themselves and the customer, making an imaginary problem real.

Align and calm yourself to be in a state of certainty. Breathe using the techniques discussed to relax your demeanor and let the words roll out of your mouth naturally.

Showing More Options to Narrow Them Down

People like to think they've looked at all options and shopped around, so they've come to the right decision and won't make a mistake. By looking around at other choices, they confirm to themselves that the choice they've made is the right one. Even if a customer was dead set on a particular product, I would still attempt to show them others.

Many times, I have seen salespeople speak to a customer who came in certain about what they wanted, only for them to walk away and not buy. A big part of this is that their mindset changed. They thought they had the sale in the bag or felt the need to protect the sale at all costs and be on hand at every given moment. This put more pressure on the customers' experience and decision-making process. Neither mentality is the correct one, as customers want to be treated with respect, and those mentalities shout desperation. People like to have the freedom to make choices in their own time and with people they can relate to and who are comfortable with themselves.

If somebody does come in looking for a certain product, accept that and treat them like you would any other customer. Still try to play devil's advocate and show them other models, still keep their why in the back of your mind to ensure that the product is right for them. This isn't being awkward; it's your moral obligation to ensure people are buying the right products. Nothing has changed just because somebody has asked for something by name, so don't let it rock your frequency and don't change your selling style to suit them.

It's almost as if you don't want the sale and are keeping it at arm's length. This may sound ludicrous, but the more you can go around the subject of closing the deal, the higher the likelihood of them making the purchase. You're building value into the product and credibility in you as a person.

It's like the sale is there for the taking, but you resist the urge to go for it. It slows the sale down and is another example of delaying gratification and playing the long game. Providing and showing all of the options available is a fantastic service that helps create confidence that the customer is making the right choice. You become the go-to salesperson for all future purchases. There is a reverse psychology element to this, but so what? When used correctly, it is so powerful, and it works.

Perhaps they will see something that they like, and that's fine. I enjoyed it when that happened, as it gave the customer something else to consider. If they did like a product and showed genuine interest, I would then engage and present the product as if they were a new customer who didn't have an idea of what they were getting. It was like we were back to square one again; all of this would still be done in a contained, enthusiastic manner. This is essential, as some customers can be quite savvy about the fact that you may be pulling a bit of a stunt. They may not say it, but there could be a look in their eyes as if to say, "So what are you going to do now?" Keeping up the act is essential, or you'll just look silly and manipulative. And in any case, if a customer is genuinely interested in the product, they deserve to be informed about it, as that's our job, right? Nine times out of ten, however, customers will go back to their original choice and be even more confident in purchasing it.

By doing this, customers would be more obliged to relent and say how they were happy with their original choice and commit to the sale without me having to say a word or close the deal. Shaolin monk Shi Heng Yi preaches that when something comes into your life that you want, you should not grab it; let it come to you naturally. The second we act out of need, want, or desperation, what we desire moves further away from us. The same goes for when you don't want something; the more you resist the subject, the more it will come back to you. It is better to accept it for what it is and deal with it accordingly.

Sometimes I would use this method to close deals when a customer was on the verge of buying but didn't necessarily have the confidence to commit. I knew that the product was a perfect fit but thought that closing could have been too strong for the situation, but they needed a gentle nudge. I would say to the customer, "I'm trying to think of other options that are suitable, but I don't think there are any." More than likely, the customer would then say, "Well, I think we've settled on this one," thus closing themselves after affirming and coming to the decision that the product is right for them.

This does sound quite passive, but every scenario is different, and sometimes you have to be more sensitive to the needs of people and their decision-making than you would somebody else. If they still don't close themselves but are showing more buying signals and are interested, categorically close the deal at this point using the phrases in the coming chapters.

Should You Stay or Should You Go?

This is the question that will make or break a salesperson's week. Should you carry on serving the customer, or should you write them off as just looking? Personally, I believe all customers are in a store for a reason to buy, whether that be today, next week, or next year.

Whenever I would serve a customer, I would do so with the exact same method I'm describing in this book. Even if a customer would say to me that they definitely aren't buying, I would still carry on serving them with, "That's fine; here are the options for X, Y, and Z." They were in the store, so I figured at some point they'd be buying in the future.

Whenever somebody showed an interest in a product, I would still add value to them and their experience and make sure not to dismiss their position. Many salespeople at this point completely lose their focus and concentration because the sale isn't happening today, but this is ludicrous; perhaps the customer just genuinely isn't in a position to buy yet. By being dismissive, these salespeople completely lose rapport and faith with their customers and run the risk of not getting the sale when they do inevitably come in to buy. They then proceed to be annoyed and angry when somebody else writes up the order! Figures, right?

I would try to tie them down, however, with a choice of what they would have if they were ready. I made sure to mention that if they did place an order "subject to change," then they would lock in the sale price that was advertised but have the advantage of changing their mind in the near future. If they agreed, then great; if not, then I'd take their number if possible and follow up with them. If this wasn't on the cards, I would write all the details down for them and, again, make it as easy as possible for them to make their purchase when they were ready to do so without being dismissive. I would always treat them with the respect and sensitivity they deserved. Many salespeople will not go this extra mile as they see it as a pointless exercise, but the amount of sales that have come back to me over the coming weeks or months that I had sown earlier made a huge difference in my quota.

Very often, a customer would tap me on the shoulder and mention how they were ready to buy and spend thousands with me. The great thing about this was that the work was already done! Sure, sometimes they'd come in on my day off and another salesperson would get them, which hurt, but that's the joy of sales. Extra for Experts: Always remember your customers! They'll feel valued, and you'll earn more money! Once the customer had the information, I left them and went onto the next one, having gotten my definitive answer that they definitely weren't buying today. This helped my energy and momentum flow easier onto the next customer, rather than me thinking about what-ifs.

The best salespeople always get an answer. Never be greedy and never try looking for the next big thing, as you could drop a diamond in the process. Concentrate and focus on what's happening in front of you with your full attention, and good things will happen. In *The Sopranos,* Michael K. Williams says, "You should'a played that out; it's the only way you gonna learn." You'll get a much better sense of job satisfaction when that customer buys from you because you had to dig deep and go that extra mile!

Chapter 7

It is a common myth that people believe closing a sale is the most important part of the process. This couldn't be further from the truth. The entire lead-up to asking for the order is equally, if not more, important. You have absolutely no right to close a deal if you haven't followed the steps prior and know that the product is right for your customer. Closing should be effortless, seamless, and the natural next step in the process. Please follow the following advice to make sure you're doing your customer a service by asking for the deal: When done correctly, customers and clients even start to close themselves.

Top Salespeople Always Get the Answer

Whether it's the answer they want is a different matter. However, the top 1% will always get an answer, either by being direct and asking it right away or by doing what I do and holding it back. The right time to ask is when there is less resistance, thus increasing the chances of getting the answer to swing in my favor.

Look at how Vito Corleone in Godfather 2 talked to the landlord who was kicking out the old woman because she had a dog. Vito gave him a spiel of how the landlord was a respectable guy; he pays the money six months in advance and offers to pay every six months because he wouldn't want the old lady to be aware as she's too proud. The landlord is taken in by the terms and looks to accept them, as Vito has handed him the money. Then Vito asks, "The dog stays, right?" Of course, the landlord didn't agree at that point, but the lead-up was to draw the person in with an offer that could have bypassed the objection. Now, Vito Corleone had other influencing factors that salespeople don't have, but we work within the confines of what we have.

Never Offer an Opinion Until You're in a Deep Level of Rapport

This is because chances are people won't trust you enough to listen to it, and it'll only raise their guard. Remember how people are hardwired to think that all salespeople are out to get them? This is a perfect example. It's irrelevant how sincere your opinion is; they don't know you, and as far as they're concerned, you're just another one of those typical closers that will tell them anything for the business. It's our job to raise our standing and be seen as equals in the customers' eyes. Playing the long game of relationship building is the only way to do it. If somebody has a color swatch and is comparing fabrics, don't just dive in and say, "I think that would be best!" Not when you're only 30 seconds into the process. It's awkward, and the timing is wrong. Uncover the why and how before any options are given, as this will ensure that you're seen as the consultant they need rather than the salesman they expect.

If you know a product isn't the right choice for them, however, note and acknowledge to them that it's a great product choice, but then explain sensitively how it may not be good for their situation based on the information you have. This isn't an opinion; these are facts that customers need to be aware of to make an informed choice. I remember once serving a customer and them telling me how they were looking for a hard-wearing sofa that was going to be used every day by the whole family and pets, only for them to then sit on and take a slight interest in one of the most impractical sofas in the store! This is why challenging the customer in a loving way helps build trust and credibility.

Challenge the Customer's Choices

This is a great way to strengthen rapport and something I've used many times to gain credibility and provide great service. Let's say, for instance, that the customer who was looking at a sofa that was impractical for their needs didn't choose an alternative and was set on their choices. I would absolutely assist them in making a choice, but early in the process, I would challenge them on their selection based on the information I had. I would say something along the lines of, "I get that you like this product but from what you've told me, I'm not too sure if it's right for your family and pets." Explain in a sensitive way why you think, based on your expertise, it may not be a great choice because of the features that the product has. Don't categorically rule out the product. If the customer loves it and they want it, as long as they're happy with any caveats that will come along, then who are you to stop them? Still, they must be made aware.

If, however, the product is totally unsuitable, then there is a moral obligation to look after the customers' welfare and have an open, transparent conversation without offending them. Show them alternatives that would be suitable, and then, at least, they can make an even more informed decision. I remember once serving a friend who needed a dining table. He came in to look at a fantastic matte-finished piece. While he was looking, I was pricing up the total, and to my surprise, he was looking at a high-gloss table that would have required a lot more upkeep. Knowing his personality traits and how he likes to keep everything clean at all times, I mentioned how he would have to be cleaning the table every day to keep it in great shape. This wasn't to put him off; it was my moral obligation to ensure that he understood the features of the product and accepted them, warts and all.

He was happy and accepted, and therefore I had to pivot my focus onto something completely different while still being enthusiastic about the product and maintaining my charisma. That inspires people to make a decision.

By asking and challenging certain customer choices, I instantly raised my standing in the customer's eyes because they realized that I did genuinely care about their purchase and the decision they would make. It also allows you to sell more insurance more easily, as with items like that, they really should sell themselves. They could either agree or disagree with me, and that was fine, but by challenging them, I protect myself from future service issues and establish a deeper level of rapport. I was also able to sleep at night knowing that I'd done everything I could for them!

For more information on how to challenge the customer's choice in a loving way, visit https://www.fromfeartomindful.com/resources/.

Be Able to Pivot

Having the ability to pivot when a customer changes their mind is essential to remaining an authority figure. Not all customers will be straightforward, and we must be flexible enough to accept this and remain agreeable with them. Providing the product is right for them, adjust your mentality to suit; don't be offended or let your enthusiasm spill over. This could mean swapping products at the last minute because a customer has had a change of heart. Perhaps they provide you with a piece of information that changes the entire scenario. You'll find, however, that most customers will look to pivot, but when you don't react emotionally, they go back to their original choice. Perhaps this could be that they are looking to you as a source of strength that brings them back into the sale rather than looking for a way out of it.

Having the Ability to Ignore

This goes for working with others and the customers you're serving. Having a thick skin and the ability to ignore what's not relevant to moving the sale forward or strengthening rapport are critical. This could be not getting involved in a conversation that a customer is having between themselves about a contentious subject, such as religion or politics. If a customer does or says something silly or contentious, having the ability to gloss over it and not make it an issue will make them feel at ease about your presence and keep you in rapport. If you do mention something, you run the risk of embarrassing them, triggering an emotional response, and losing future sales. People have long-term memories, and when you offend them, they'll remember how you made them feel. This could create awkward exchanges in the future. It's best to stay away from things like that. Always leave the door open for future business. The desire for the business should outweigh anything else.

Intent is Your Best Friend

Studies show that there are much greater chances of customers spending more money when intent is applied to them, which means making them feel as if they're the only ones in the room and not just a number. Another study showed that when a waiter left mints with the bill for his customers, he would receive a certain level of tip. However, when the same waiter giving the same bill and mints started to walk away and then spun on his heels, turned back around to his customers, and gave an extra mint each, the waiter received a considerably higher tip. Yes, there is a certain amount of showmanship involved in this, but that's how customer service works. How can you apply this to your working environment?

Once, I went to an older customer's house to measure and see if a sofa would fit in their living room, taking the pressure off them to do it themselves. This may seem like a common practice to some stores, but this was a large national corporate chain that didn't offer this kind of service, and it was unorthodox for me to do so. This kind of intent is what's needed in order to create a relationship that's everlasting.

Have the intent of booking all business that walks through your door, no matter the customer. Every person enters your floor for a reason. Remember that.

Compliment Only When it's Sincere and Genuine

Paying a compliment to a customer is a great way to clinch a deal, but it must be said in a genuine and sincere way. I would never go as far as saying how clever they were or try to "brown-nose" them around to my way of thinking to butter them up into making a decision. If I thought a product would look fantastic in their setting, however, I'd mention it to them. Very often, customers would show me pictures of their rooms, and I could visualize how the layout would be. I'd get excited for them and say, "I think this will look awesome" or "I love that idea; what about this?" Then I'd go on to suggest a thought that I had.

At this stage, you're at a deep enough level of rapport to have an opinion that's valued by the customer and not seen as a flippant comment. It also gives you a great insight into what other products will go into the room, and you can suggest them too! Really go to town and let your inner interior designer come out while remaining contained and enthusiastic. Customers love this, as you're really getting involved in the process and will value your passion and thoughts. It'll only make the customer trust you more and inspire them to shop with you now and in the future. Even mention to a customer something similar to, "You look really comfortable on that!" If it's truly the case, this could inspire them to decide.

Be Their Biggest Fan

This kind of contradicts what I've just said, slightly. Whenever a customer mentions how they've made a bad choice in the past or how they're talking down to themselves in any way, be there to pick them back up again.

Don't brown-nose them, but support them by showing genuine empathy. Mention something like, "You did your best with the knowledge available" or say something like, "You weren't to blame" for a scenario that happened. 1) This is the correct practice for any human being who is feeling low within themselves. 2) Customers will trust you more as you've shown vulnerability by sincerely looking after their needs and welfare.

This will only strengthen and deepen the rapport you're building, creating a stronger sales relationship.

Start To Paint The Picture

Throughout the sales process, as you're proactively overcoming objections and demonstrating the features and benefits of products, you'll get a feel for what's right for the customer and what isn't. By moving on from the conversation and acknowledging that somebody likes a particular feature, you're allowing the customer to build up a picture in their mind that they want to buy the product. This is playing the long game of sales, but it's a much classier, consultive encounter. It's very similar to leaving a trail of breadcrumbs and hoping that somebody will pick up the trail and follow it straight to the cash register.

There shouldn't be a need to close every little detail as this can become extremely tedious and can be very short-sighted. An example of this is, "Okay, so you like the shade of red, yes? Now what about the size?" This method is micromanaging the customer and not allowing them to think freely. It's our job to help create an environment that is seamless, rather than regimented. Try something similar to this once somebody has chosen a color, "Nice, that'll look great. Have you got a 3str or a 2str?" This is a seamless conversation that flows much better.

When asking about sizes, try to stick to asking questions that people will know the answer to. This makes them feel confident about themselves and reinforces positivity. An example of this is instead of asking what size somebody needs, ask whether they have a 2 or 3 seater sofa at present. Not many people will know the actual dimensions of their sofa but most will know how many it seats. If they're looking at a sofa with narrower arms that seats the same amount of people, you know it'll fit. This works the same with dining furniture.

There are occasions however where you have got to be more assertive as some customers genuinely can't decide for themselves. In this scenario demonstrating a more micro-managed approach is more appropriate but ensure that it's in an assertive but non aggressive manner.

Making the Choice

As professionals, we must always keep an eye on the proceedings of the sale and, when in a deep enough level of rapport, offer an opinion based on facts. When it comes down to a choice based on preference, however, we must resist the urge to get involved. It's the choice and decision of the customer that really matter. I used to absolutely hate giving opinions on preferences such as products or colors, and I still hate to get involved now. Even when they wanted my opinion, I'd try my best to refrain from giving it: I'd say to the customer that it's not my decision in a warm, empathetic manner and give them the pros and cons of each choice. I was purely there to help them make that decision with informed judgment.

I would help them narrow their choices down, however, by asking which were the front runners. I'd then get rid of other choices that were available if the customer clearly wasn't as interested in them. This influenced their decision while keeping them in a position of authority. I'd even sit down and ask for details about the room decor and visualize how the layout would take shape. What color scheme is there? Is there a feature wall? Is it a room that brings in lots of natural sunlight? Then I'd throw in suggestions and comments to try to get the creative juices flowing from the customer. This is a perfect example of what I call "leading by not leading." As salespeople, we're leading the sale, but we're doing it in a way that will entice the customer to use their own gray matter to make a decision rather than having it made for them.

By helping them make decisions on their own terms, customers are much more confident and satisfied with their purchases. It's a much more intelligent way of serving customers, and it leaves them more content. Not everybody has the same thought process when it comes to making decisions; some make them quicker than others, and that's fine. We must accept that and be patient and sensitive to their needs. By always playing the long game, remembering that future relationship, and not doing anything to jeopardize it, we'll win. Customers will keep coming back time after time as you've shared a strong intimate experience together. I mean, you've literally just sat down in their house; you can't get more personal than that!

As salespeople, you need to play your part in that decision and immerse yourself in the customer's solutions without over-trading the mark. You need to treat it less as a transaction or a me vs. you mentality and turn it into a team game in which you're on the same side of the table. Make choices for the greater good. The minute you come across as being salesy to customers, you've lost rapport and the relationship. You have to fall in love with your customers and their solution; only then will your true intentions come through. Staying neutral at all times lets the customer make decisions for themselves, lowering sales resistance. Still, there was the odd time I'd offer an opinion, but it would only be as a last resort for a customer who genuinely couldn't do it by them-selves.

When there's a deep level of rapport, opinions carry more weight. At this stage, we're seen as genuine, honest, and sincere, just like the opinion we're offering, and not just using it as a ploy to make the customer come to a quicker decision. However, it would still be given while metaphorically treading a tad lightly, as it's still ultimately their decision and their money they're spending.

If the time came and I had to cave and give my view to move the sale forward, I'd give my thoughts on what I think would go best by giving a safer, more blended option that doesn't offend and a complete contrast of color to bring the room to life and create a talking point, if it was appropriate. If there were hints of green in the feature wall. Why not the same green sofa? Then tie in the neutral colors as cushions to provide a homelier look.

Giving two options makes it easier for customers to decide, as people love to have choices to affirm they're making the right one. This is because they just want to confirm to themselves that they've made the right decision. Whatever my opinions, though, they had to be genuine. When picking a contrasting color, it would have to be one that I thought would suit the room. I'd never make a thoughtless comment that didn't add value. Even if the customer thought I was a little off my rocker for picking such colors, that was fine; I'd stand by my own choice because it was genuinely my thoughts! Nine times out of ten, the customers would then pick the safer option or the option they had originally leant towards, but having a conversation about it helped sway them.

Let's take a second to reflect...

So, we've just discussed how we should almost act as an interior designer for our customers, recommending relevant products and services that will enhance their experience. What about pre-packaging bundles that customers can buy to make the process even easier? When selling a three- and two-seater sofa, offer a footstool at half price if bought in the highest-grade leather. When selling a carpet, offer a platinum package where you provide the best service, including top-quality and new accessories such as underlay door rails, fitting, uplift, and removal. What about vacuuming and moving furniture as a standard too?

All of this is built into the price, but when proposed as a package, people will be more inclined to buy. If you're selling bikinis, offer a free bottle of quality sun-tan lotion or something similar if a customer buys three sets or more. People always go for the easier, more obvious option, so why not provide that option for them? Even if just one in ten takes you up on the offer, it's an increase in sales for no extra work. Again, try not to discount as such but rather build value in the product and your services by adding to the order.

Every year, I take a select few students and help them Double Your Sales With Half The Stress In 2 Years Or Less, Guaranteed. Seventy-five percent of the fee is linked to results. Fair enough?

If you'd like to apply, see if you'd be a good fit. Contact me by the means below:

info@fromfeartominful.com

www.linkedin.com/in/sam-king-from-fear-to-mindful/

I also offer a great referral incentive to anyone who refers a salesperson or company that may benefit from this program and gets through the application process.

On the Verge of Buying

When you know a customer is nearly ready to place an order, ask them, "Why is this 'Product X' the right fit? What other colors or accent tones must it complement? How will it look in the room? Is it the right color and style?" This gets the customer to justify to themselves why the product is right for them; they're painting a picture in their mind that this is the product that they'll be having. It's also your moral obligation to ensure the product is the right choice for them, so by asking, you're fulfilling your duty. Once a customer has justified to themselves how it will work and that it's a great choice, more often than not they close themselves. If not, simply close the deal. While you could just straight up ask, "Why do you think this is a good choice?" Personally, I think this is a little sleazy and salesy, rather than coming from a consultative point of view.

Delivering the Price

Always be extra focused when pricing products for a customer. If you give the wrong price, at a minimum, it looks unprofessional, but at worst, it could mean you lose an order. Here's an example of how I learned the hard way to stay focused when pricing goods for customers: I was pricing a corner suite up one time, and it came to what I thought was around $3,400. The customer went away to "think about it" and then came in a few days later to buy. I worked around the prices, and to my shock, I had underpriced it by about $300. The customer wasn't impressed, and as there was nowhere to move on price, the customer ultimately walked out in a very bad mood, and rightly so, which killed the relationship. I also missed out on my target for the period by about $3000. Ouch. It was a mistake that haunted me for months, and I even mentioned to my sales manager how it would never happen again.

Luckily, it never did happen again because I double and triple checked every order that had the potential to go wrong—I even double checked the straightforward ones! When working in a store with a product specification card, I would write down the price on the card and give it to the customer. This is unusual, as they were expecting to be closed at this point, but instead they received a card for them to take away. I did this because many customers would say to me, "Write that down for me, and we'll think about it."

Already writing it down and giving it to them disarmed the objection, lowered sales resistance, and showed pure transparency.

When I wrote the details down, I would verbalize the details to the customer by writing out what was chosen before giving it to them. I would then let the customer read the card and ask them, "Shall we do it?"

Normally, the price is the last hurdle to get over before an order is placed. This was my subtle take on the "Summary Close," where you summarize what the customer has looked at and then ask for the order. By doing this, however, it was done in a much more relaxed way, as it was being written down for the customers to take away rather than a hard close. It also gives them an opening to give final objections such as, "Great, we'll take that and go to measure up, etc." That's your cue for the subject to close. Say something like, "We're able to take an order subject to size. If it fits, great, just call me and I can release the order, if not we can look at alternatives or offer a refund no questions asked." If you haven't got a spec card then I suggest you get one, as it will work wonders.

When closing, the tonality needs to be the exact same as what you've been using all the way through your presentation. A casual tone while being direct and assertive creates a seamless exchange for the customer. Speak in a manner that insinuates that everybody buys at this stage; it's the natural next step. This will give most customers the confidence to agree with you.

A Little White Lie Won't Hurt

No, I'm not saying you should lie to your customers. I'm saying that telling your managers and colleagues a white lie is fine sometimes. Very often, when I had a bite of a big sale, a nosey consultant or manager who wanted a sale on the books would ask me if they were buying and want me to commit myself. I would almost always tell them, "No, not today," and completely play down the fact that I was almost certain they were buying.

The reason I did this was because if I had said that they were buying, I would have released my contained enthusiasm, and when I then went back to interact with the customer, there would have been a subtle difference in my demeanor. If you commit, you're no longer in a state of surrender. You then start to emit "push energy" rather than letting the scenario play out by itself. These little differences make all the difference, and my focus had to be at 100% all the time to be the top salesperson. So, the next time your manager or nosey colleague wants to know what's happening with your sales funnel, don't be shy about telling them a white lie. They certainly won't mind if they book.

Address the Hesitation

If there is hesitation from the customer or if something seems a little off when it's nearly time to close the deal, you must address it before you close. If you don't, you'll only put the customer under more pressure, which will increase their chances of walking. Even if they do buy, you'll ruin the relationship and increase the chances of buyers' remorse. Always make sure there is complete clarity on a subject before moving on to the next step. I would address the hesitation with sentences such as, "You seem a little unsure or hesitant about it; what's holding you back?" Or something as simple as giving a statement like, "You seem a little hesitant…" People should be treated courteously, and if their feelings matter, who knew in sales this had to be the case, right? By doing this, more than likely the customer will tell you their objections, whether that be time restrictions, price, or something else. Once we get the objections, we have something to work with and can start to move the sale along. Never be frightened of hearing an objection. Objections mean the customer wants to buy the product but is coming up with ideas not to; it's simply our job to overcome these as seamlessly as possible while keeping our cool.

For more information on how to address hesitation, visit https://www.fromfeartomindful.com/resources/.

Closing the Sale

This should come naturally, provided you've put in the work prior and really delved deep into the needs of the customer. By now, the customer is calm, relaxed, and ready to make a final decision. Hopefully they've already decided and closed with themselves which is the best scenario to be in. You'll know that they're ready when they're happy and content with their choices.

Making a decision is the obvious next step. You can only close once you know the product is right for them and have full confidence that they'll be happy with their purchase. If there is any hesitation, then you must address it. Under no circumstances should you close if there is hesitation or something in the back of your mind that needs to be brought to their attention.

When it gets to the stage of closing the deal and the customer hasn't closed themselves during the presentation stage, as a sales professional, you simply must ask the question, as it's your moral obligation.

Many times, when I closed with a customer for the first time, the deal was done. But in reality, it was done because of the work I'd put into the front end of the sale; closing was just a formality. Customers may not want to hear you close, but they need to hear it. The second you do it, even if they reject it, which there is still a very small chance of, you will feel confident in yourself, and the customer will feel more confident in you too. What would have been the point of giving a fantastic presentation and providing great service for the past hour to then leave a customer hanging? Customers want to buy; that's why they've come into the store. They don't come in to kill time or waste time; okay, maybe some, but the majority want to buy products, and it's our professional duty to carry out that process right up to the very end. Don't do your customer a disservice by not asking for the sale. Eighty percent of good salespeople don't hit their quota. Why? Because they don't ask for the sale. Say the words over and over to yourself to get more confident in the way they roll off your tongue. Try role-playing with somebody who is willing to help you out, maybe a colleague, and then reverse roles. Practice makes absolute perfect, and the more you do it, the more confident you'll be saying it in real life and the more natural you'll sound.

Naturally, I served customers to the best of my ability and bent over backwards for them. I'm a giver. The issue I had at the start was that I struggled to find the confidence to ask for the order. Which is ridiculous to say since I gave all the help during the presentation! At times, this resulted in them coming back to the store another time and booking with somebody else. Put yourself in the customers' shoes; you've just spent an hour explaining their situation for you to sit gawping at them when they're clearly ready to buy. It's not fair for them to be the first ones to instigate the conversation because you're the one scared of being vulnerable and rejected. It also completely contradicts the constant of you being that authority figure that the customers need. If you've asked how the product will look in its setting and they think it's a great choice, it's a no-brainer to then ask for the order, provided all you've heard is positive feedback. More than likely, they'll make the decision themselves.

When I was younger, my grandad would come around every Thursday as it was "pay day." He would give me about £2 pocket money, provided I asked him for it. I'd sit with him in awkward silence every Thursday evening, and after a while, he'd say to me, "What day is it?" I'd shrug my shoulders and tell him I didn't know, even though I knew very well what day it was. He'd then tell me how I did know and that I had to ask, regardless of how I felt. I was scared of asking and looking foolish; I didn't have the confidence. The same is true in sales, but this time I'd earned the right to ask, so why not ask? Not to mention, the customer deserves to be closed.

Dan Lok says, "Closing is not something that you do for something. Closing is something that you do for somebody." Jay Abraham even says that "people are silently begging to be led." Brian Tracy mentioned how some savvy realtors would walk back to the car and mention to the prospects, "Do you like the house?"

The customer would reply, "Yes." So, they would ask, "Why don't you put in an offer?" This is such a simple close, but it works as long as you have the confidence to do so. They provided their customers with the exact service that was needed and took the pressure off them. I would do something very similar when closing products in store too, such as asking, "Do you like it?" or "Do you think they would look good in the room?" The answer will obviously be yes. Then I'd respond, "Ok, nice, shall we do it?"

You won't upset anybody by asking, especially if you've followed the steps. It shouldn't be a big formal occasion, with you rolling out the red carpet while you're asking for the order. Sometimes simple, casual lines such as "Shall we do it?" or "Shall we start the paperwork?" are more than enough. Sometimes a customer mentioned that they needed more time to decide, so I happily gave it to them. I'd acknowledge the fact that it was a "big decision" and that they have all the time they need to make it the right one. The customer will start to respect you more when you close the deal. You've proven to them and yourself how much of a professional you really are, even if they aren't quite ready to give you an answer yet because of scenarios such as a hidden objection or because they need more time. Only do this if it's right to close; if not, you'll look like a pushy salesperson, which isn't what we want.

Sometimes customers would take a little longer than others to decide. Depending on the level of rapport and relationship I had with them by the third close, I'd have a joke with them and say something along the lines of, "Haven't you made your mind up yet? Come on!" in a joking way, making sure my contained enthusiasm didn't spill over into arrogance. This only threw me into a deeper level of rapport, as I could be playful and not take the whole process so seriously.

Buying products, whether they be cars, carpets, or furniture, doesn't have to be an ordeal. The more pressure you can take away from the customers' experience, the stronger the relationship you'll have. When a customer would ask, "What do we do next?" I would simply answer, "We just need to do some paperwork" or "We just need some signatures." These were very informal, casual lines that lowered sales resistance and their guard. Under no circumstances say that they've got to sign a contract or anything else that just screams sales. That would build up resistance and hinder the chances of adding or selling additional products.

Always think of the interaction with a customer as a long-term relationship rather than a singular transaction. Treat your customers as if they were yours forever and that you were the go-to person from now on for all future purchases. This will ease the pressure of asking for the sale, as the interaction technically hasn't finished and there will be more sales to come!

For extra information on how to close a deal, go to https://www.fromfeartomindful.com/resources/.

We Want to Think About It

How many times have you heard this? You've exhausted yourself, only for a customer to then say how they need to think about it. It was almost there for the taking, and now it's gone from your grasp, or so it seems! Whenever a customer says that they want to think about it, under no circumstances should you let your emotions spill or bubble over. I would say, "Of course, I'll write the details down for you." I would then proceed to write down all the possible details of the product they had chosen, making it as easy as possible for them when they next came in. This would show the customer that I wasn't desperate or needed the sale, and it would keep me in a position of authority.

I would never write my name down on the card, as I felt that by doing that I was trying to own the sale rather than let it come back to me freely. Whenever I wrote my name down or asked a customer to ask for me, and they didn't, it annoyed me and shook my energy. This then caused my frequency to spike, and I was out of kilter for a period of time, thus affecting my day.

As far as I was concerned, if I was meant to have the order, then it would come back to me; if I wasn't, then it wouldn't. This may sound like a holistic approach, but by unconditionally giving it to the universe, it does have a way of coming back to you.

It also helped that I had and still have a fantastic memory and could recognize customers that I had served months or even years before. It goes without saying that living a clean life helps with this. I would then give the details to the customer and ask them, "What was it you needed to think about?" They would then reveal their objections again, if there were any, whether that be delivery times, prices, size constraints, or perhaps they had not seen other products at a competitor. Again, this is an opportunity to overcome these objections; never be afraid of them. More often than not, customers would relent and just buy the product.

Sometimes a person needs to be put on the spot in order to make a choice. This was softer, as we had the specification cards to use as a tool to soften the blow of closing business. It gave them something to hold onto almost like a comfort blanket and allowed them feel that there was no pressure. It was also a constant, as I had been doing this through the entire presentation, so it wasn't out of character for me to be useful in such a way. If you don't have a spec card to provide, I suggest that when somebody says they want to think about it, you simply say, "Of course, what was it you wanted to think about?" Go through the process again. Say "What was it?" rather than "What is it?" By doing this, you're detaching yourself from the sale, making it easier to entice people to open up. It's a reflective question that shows you're interested but not desperate, rather than a direct question that could, and most likely will, put customers on the spot and raise sales resistance.

Never stop a customer from looking elsewhere; it only comes across as needy and desperate and could be quite aggressive. Whenever somebody mentioned how they were going to look elsewhere, I would never argue or debate with them; I simply accepted it, even though underneath I was disappointed. If the product they were looking at was a brand that was widely available, I'd say that we could price match any other quotes. If the product was exclusive to us, I didn't say anything, because if they fell in love with the product, they'd be back. This is similar to not asking a customer to ask for me by name to give me a referral; I let the universe decide whether they were going to come back to me or not rather than forcing the point. All I could do was give my very best, lay all the information out for the customer to acknowledge, and then let them make their own mind up. As far as I was concerned, they had walked, and the order had gone. It was my job to close people there and then, rather than having to rely on comebacks coming back into store to make my week. This is where so many salespeople go wrong. Never rely on "should've," "would've," or "could've," rather than dealing with what's happening in the here and now. If they do come back in, then that's a bonus, but never rely on them to.

If a customer didn't ask for me and somebody else wrote up the order before I recognized them, then I wrote it off as collateral. As hard as it is, there's nothing more you can do. Just accept it and move on to the next customer. If it's so busy that you didn't recognize them, there are more orders to be had, but try to be sharper next time. If it was quiet and you didn't recognize them, then unfortunately, you only have yourself to blame.

For more information on how to handle this objection, go to https://www.fromfeartomindful.com/resources/.

Know Your Competition

Knowing what you're up against is vital in order to win sales. This could be regarding offers, products, or other tools in their box that they're using against you. The more you know about them, the more you're able to maneuver around them. Take this example, for instance: One day I was serving a customer who was buying a configuration of leather sofas. They then mentioned to me that they were going to look next door. I said that was fair enough and didn't stop them from looking, as this would raise resistance. I did mention, however, that all of our sofas were 100% leather front, back, and sides as a standard, whereas the competitor only showed them on the fronts of the sofa. The rest, upholstered in hide, would have been an extra cost at the desk. I wasn't talking down to the competitor or their products; I was simply stating a fact that the customer should look out for. Sure enough, 10 minutes later, they came back in and bought. No, I didn't bring up the leather options; I simply accepted they were back to buy and left the point unspoken.

The Subject to Close

Taking an order subject to size or color is the best way to nail down a customer who cannot physically make a certain decision at a particular moment, especially with higher-ticket items. Perhaps they really do need to measure; perhaps they really have left their credit card at home. Taking an order subject to where a customer does have an option of cancelling within the next 48-72 hours if certain criteria aren't met, has made me so much commission and I can't get why some salespeople or companies don't use it. If somebody is willing to leave you a deposit, then the chances are that they are serious about their purchase. I can count on one hand the people who have cancelled after closing an order subject to change. While serving customers is our priority, we must never allow ourselves to be taken advantage of. Say, for instance, that a customer is undecided on two colors; you may offer to order them a sample of each for them to choose in their own home, providing they pay a refundable deposit. This stops you from losing a sale and wasting your time. Ask them, "Is it just a case of choosing a color? If so, we can write up an order, subject to change based on color, and then order you a sample. If you're not completely happy with the choice, we can look at alternatives or, of course, offer a full refund."

Obviously this is a last resort as a concrete sale is more preferable. But why leave anything off the table, especially when it's only a case of ironing out finer details?

Could I Take Your Contact Details?

If a customer wasn't willing to leave a deposit subject to change, I would always ask for their contact details to follow up with them after they had completed whatever task they had to undertake. These then went into my own diary, which I checked every morning for who and what I had to chase and a little description to remind me of the subject. Sometimes on a busy weekend, I would take a customer's number and then say, "I'll call you at the start of next week to see if it works, probably Monday or Tuesday."

This little show of ambiguity proved that I wasn't desperate for the sale by creating a gray area. Then, when next week came around, I would call them, at the earliest, on Monday afternoon or even push it back to Tuesday morning or afternoon. I would never call them at first light on Monday morning, as this would just show desperation and come across as a typical salesperson. Very often, a customer would say to me, "Oh, I thought you would have called earlier." This only lowered sales resistance even more, making them feel more comfortable buying.

Whenever I phoned them, I wouldn't start the conversation by asking how their day was or similar small talk. I would say something along the lines of, "Hi, 'Mr. X', it's Sam from Kings Carpets; did you manage to measure up your area to see if 'Product Y' would fit?" This is getting straight to the point of the phone call, which is what the customer needs; they know you're not interested in their day or anything else, so just get straight to it while being polite. I'd then leave it with them, and depending on the answer, I would either arrange a time to call them back if they hadn't, close the deal, or overcome the objections that were brought up.

Whenever I booked a call, I would never give anybody a certain time slot. I would always try to give a time of between 2-4 p.m., for example, or after 3, as I was busy and didn't want to either be late or let the customer down when I didn't call them. This also gave the impression that my time was valuable. I wasn't just available on a whim for anybody at any given time; I was a busy salesperson, and we had to find a time that fit in with both of our schedules. I'd explain this to the customers too when booking the call: that I'd be serving customers and would probably be busy, so I wouldn't be able to give a time.

If I was pressed to give a specific time, I would always call one to two minutes after the time scheduled to show I wasn't desperate or needy. For example, if I said I would call at 6:00 p.m. I would call at 6:01 p.m., 6:02 p.m., etc. If somebody at this point isn't willing to hand over their contact details, then simply accept that that's the end of the process and politely wish them a good day after providing all the details to make it as easy as possible if they do come in the future.

Negotiation

With commodity items found in retail stores, there will always be people who want a discount. I have researched many sales books, and the vast majority conclude that even when a price has been lowered, it doesn't necessarily mean it'll sell more. Very often, the conversation rates stay exactly the same. This tells us that price is not the main driver for the sale, but how people perceive the value is. This is why it's important not to collapse when a customer asks for a discount. In retail, salespeople need to prepare themselves for the fact that the customer is going to ask for a discount, as it's more or less inevitable. Once you get your mindset right after giving the price and building that slight wall of resilience, your answers will come from a much more confident position. Here are a few tips to help you get over the hurdle of discounting:

Acting Surprised

When a customer asks for a discount, simply raise your eyebrows and act a little surprised. Then proceed to tell the customer, "I'm sorry, we can't do that." Some salespeople will give a straight-up no or say something like, "We don't discount." I've seen it work extremely well for them. Personally, it's a little too abrupt for my liking, but everybody's different.

How Do You Mean?

By asking this question you put the customer on the back foot when they ask for a discount. When they give you their reply, simply say: "We don't discount." If a customer is relentless and still persists then either of the phrases below would work.

'If I Can .... Will You...?'

This phrase gets a commitment from the customer that if you do what is asked, they'll be willing to place an order. Here's an example: "If I can take off $50, will you be placing the order today? If I can add free delivery and installation to your order, will you be making the purchase?" If the answer is a resounding yes, then proceed to ask a manager. If the answer is no, then don't bother, as it will be a waste of your time. Let them think that you're working hard for them to have this deal and that they aren't given out willy-nilly.

How Much Do You Think Would Be Fair?

This phrase instantly puts the spotlight back on the customer and lets them think of a figure. If you feel that it's appropriate, then use "if I can, will you," but if not, then simply let them know that you can't do that. When talking about prices, discounts, or any negotiation, keeping your enthusiasm contained is vital to managing the interaction. Of course, there are the obvious signs, such as saying something you shouldn't, but there are also more subtle clues that you need to watch out for.

Laughing or smiling nervously is a big factor in keeping your contained enthusiasm and these behaviors must be managed in order to remain the authority figure. This is something that took me years to figure out, but I finally got it by keeping a straight face and focusing on moving the sale forward in the customer's time. Never be domineering in your approach. Knowing when to keep a straight face and not take the bait of reacting emotionally is critical if you want to keep the upper hand in the negotiation. The fact is, with retail sales, people can afford the items they're looking at. If they couldn't, they wouldn't have spent the time and effort going through the entire presentation, opening up about how and why the product would be great for them. The prices are clear for everybody to see, right? So, whenever somebody mentions how they can't afford it, more often than not, it's a ruse to get a further discount on the product.

Add-ons

Add-ons are essential for business growth and, more importantly, for providing the customer with great service. Look at add-ons as an extra package that will only enhance the customer's experience, rather than something you need to check a box for. The majority of add-ons are either there to enhance the life and longevity of a product or to act as accessories and bring to life what they've already bought. Always assume that the customer doesn't have what you need, and therefore it's your moral obligation to ensure that all possible extras are brought to their attention. Never sell an add-on before the bulk of the order has been confirmed; this will only push customers away, and never try to sell two items at the same time. Always close the first item before moving onto the second. This ensures the customer has a perfect focus on each product individually and gives them a greater chance of having it. Once you've closed the bulk of the order, be excited for them as they've made a purchase! Then use phrases like, "What about the....? They create the entire look."

"Have you got a...? I recommend you have a new one for your new..."

Examples could be:

"What about the cushions? They create the entire look."

"Have you got a door rail? I recommend everybody have a new one with every new carpet."

In furniture showrooms, there is a reason the best ones are laid out like you're walking into somebody's living area. There are rugs, coffee tables, lamps, and sofas to sit on. All of these accessories should complement each other and bring the entire look together. People should get a sense of how their living area could be, and it's our job as salespeople to bring this to their attention. Selling the room rather than the product expands the customer's mind to think about what else they can buy. Simply state, "Did you see this?" You'll bring items to the attention of customers, and the chance of further purchases being made will increase.

Additional Items

Once a customer has made up their mind, always ask if there is anything else you could help them with. If they're moving houses, recommend furniture for another room, as more than likely they'll need something. If they're buying a new carpet, why not recommend that they have new blinds or drapes that complement the colors? Offering a 10% voucher for any additional items that are bought in store with a purchase is a great incentive to encourage a customer to buy more products. Many times, I have spoken with a customer who has originally come into the store to buy one item, only to then buy further items for other rooms simply by asking a question and putting the idea forward to them. Once somebody is in a buying mood, keep going until they tell you to stop; never lose your composure.

Realize that you're in fact doing the customer a service by helping them buy their products and goods at the same time, all under one roof. This makes it easier to organize delivery times and dates; you'll be the only person they have to call regarding any questions or issues that arise instead of having to deal with other people and companies. Perhaps they want to finance the goods, and this can be rolled into one payment as opposed to many payments and finance agreements having to be created. Even if I spoke with a customer who mentioned straight off the bat that they were looking for multiple items, I would suggest that we get "Product X" sorted first, then move onto other items. This gave my customers the focus they needed to make a clear choice before moving onto other pieces. Whenever there are too many options in the air at once, you run the risk of losing the entire sale. Break it down into palatable pieces that make it simple to understand. The customers will appreciate it. Have you heard of "KISS?" It stands for "Keep It Simple, Stupid!"

"If you have a product that delivers value, you have a moral obligation to reach as many people as you can." - Jay Abraham

Previous Bad Experiences

Sometimes customers would show a little hesitation and explain how they'd been let down in the past by other competitors. In this case, I'd explain that "companies are seen for what they are when things don't go to plan. I'm not going to sit here and say that everything is perfect, because sometimes hiccups do happen. What I can assure you of, though, is that I will be all over everything. If anything does happen, I'll call and keep you in the loop at all times. I'm only a phone call away if you need anything; is that okay?" This would always put customers' minds at ease and make them feel comfortable carrying on with the paperwork.

The Deal is Done

Always shake the hands of all parties involved and express how much you appreciate them, their time, and how much it's valued. Mention to them that if they need anything else, they can just call or pop in at any time to see you. Provide them with a further voucher to incentivize them. This could be monetary, such as providing a free product with additional purchases, etc. Always comment on how they've made a fantastic purchase and that you're truly happy for them. Carry any items that they've purchased to their vehicle for them, follow up on or make notes of any additional tasks you promised you would when you said you would, then proceed onto the next customer! Remember to always compose yourself before the next interaction to stay present and focused!

Asking for Referrals

Personally, I would never straight up ask for a referral, as I believe that the second you do, the fantastic service that you've provided has been squandered for personal gain. Referrals should be on a "give to get" basis, and therefore, if a customer is going to refer you, something needs to be in it for them. This separates the referral from the service you've provided, as fantastic service should be a benchmark, not used as leverage for future business. The best referral you can ever receive is an unsolicited referral, and these customers must be treated like rock stars. Nevertheless, all referral business, whether solicited or not, must be treated with the utmost respect. Have you seen the video of Simon Sinek talking about his financial advisor? He called Simon up to "congratulate" him on his house move. In reality, however, it was purely a task for a referral. Simon realized this and mentioned he would never do business with him again, let alone refer him.

Keep the Momentum Going!

Great! You've booked the order; now get onto the next one. Use this confidence to springboard you onto the next customer. Make sure you stay in the zone, keep your enthusiasm from spilling over, and channel your focus into the present. Don't stand talking with colleagues, showing off about how much commission you've earned, or going to check your phone; keep the energy flowing. If you're hungry and there are customers, let the adrenaline of selling sustain you until the customers subside, rather than going for lunch! I appreciate that a doctor might not agree with me, but that's the nature of the beast! Sales can be feast or famine, literally!

"Momentum solves 80% of your problems."
- John C Maxwell

Another Chance to Double Your Sales with Half I Stress...

I mentioned how I would never ask for a referral directly, which is true. I would, however, use a method that is classy and non-pushy and that only elevates your value in the customer's eyes, and that's called The Envelope Method. This is on a "give to get" basis. After extensive testing, studies have found that the sweet spot for any referral to be made after a customer has purchased is 48 hours. After that, they've forgotten about you. Well, maybe not quite, but that's the sweet spot. This means that you must provide your customer with a beautifully crafted envelope within the 48-hour window. This could be delivered by FedEx the following day or perhaps provided to the customer at the point of sale as a token gesture to be opened when they get home.

Inside the envelope should be a beautifully written, hand-crafted letter that states something like this:

Dear (Insert First Name),

Thank you so much for contributing to becoming a member of the (Insert Business Name) family! You're a valued member of our family, and we wanted to say, "Thanks for believing in us." We look forward to continuing a long and mutually prosperous relationship. One of our guiding principles is that to help us grow and find more people just like you, we'd rather reward our existing clients than spend money on advertising with strangers or social media companies. Our favorite way to find great new clients is through referrals from our existing clients. We know what makes an ideal client (someone like you!) and how to honor and respect that. As a result, we have a quick favor to ask of you. If you are able to help out, we would love to treat you and a friend to lunch at (Insert Restaurant Name). Take a moment to complete the attached referral sheet, take a photo with your cell phone, and text it to my personal cell at (Insert Cell Phone Number) or email it to (Insert Email Address), and if any of them become clients, we will treat the two of you to lunch as a way of saying thanks. Either way, thank you for your business! We look forward to meeting new friends! Warmest personal regards,

(Your Name)

(Business Name)

P.S. It means even more that you've chosen to believe in us in 2023. With all the chaos going on across the globe and at home, we plan to continue to honor that decision. At any point in time, if we drop the ball, you have my personal cell phone number. Please give me a call or shoot me a text, okay? :-)

Send this to all your clients, and just think of all the extra revenue you'll create. If you're a salesperson, this can be adjusted to the level of commission you're on. In virtually all cases, it is the gesture that counts rather than the monetary value that is given. There are next to no salespeople offering this kind of referral scheme, so if you apply it to your business, you'll easily increase your revenue exponentially and with ease.

Extra for Experts: Cut a deal with the restaurant so you get a meal at half price, as they're going to be receiving more revenue from you. Provide them with a leaflet rack to give to their customers too.

Every year I take a select few students and help them Double Your Sales With Half The Stress In 2 Years Or Less, Guaranteed. Seventy-five percent of the fee is linked to results. Fair enough?

If you'd like to apply, see if you'd be a good fit. Contact me by the means below:

info@fromfeartomindful.com

www.linkedin.com/in/sam-king-from-fear-to-mindful/

I also offer a great referral incentive to anyone who refers a salesperson or company that may benefit from this program and gets through the application process.

Chapter 8

If you're working in an environment where everybody gets along and there's no drama, then I am truly happy for you. I'm particularly impressed with your managers and leaders, as this is where grievances and rifts between staff should be nipped in the bud. I commend their strength and ability to handle the situation. However, more than likely, this isn't the case, and this is especially true in sales! Wherever there are targets, accountability, and, of course, commission involved, there is room for underhanded behaviors, and you need to be constantly vigilant. Remember, these are salespeople you're dealing with, and the majority would sell their own mother-in-law for a quick buck. This doesn't mean you should adopt the same behavioral patterns to be successful.

Quite the opposite, not getting involved in petty arguments or tiffs will increase your confidence and help you remain in a consistent emotional state. If you're new to a company, then obviously you'll have no idea how the system works and need to figure it out as quickly as possible. You'll be wide-eyed to begin with, but sooner or later you'll start to get and accept people's behavioral patterns. When a scenario inevitably arises where another salesperson has trod on your toes or vice versa regarding customers or any other matter, address it in a positive manner and try to come to an agreement. You'll find out whether they're reasonable or not, and you'll be able to adapt your future behavior to suit.

Many stores will have their own rules for day-to-day politics, and these should be adhered to. It's your responsibility to be accountable and assert yourself when other sales professionals don't adhere to these rulings, whether knowingly or unknowingly. Perhaps it's a genuine mistake, perhaps not. Sooner or later, you'll realize who is to be trusted and who isn't. This isn't malicious; it's just a fact that some people are opportunistic, while others are more receptive to being straight and working together. It could take days, weeks, or even months to get and accept peoples' mentalities and behaviors because you're green to the floor, but you'll get there as long as you stay keen to your surroundings and learn from what people tell you and what their actions dictate.

Hopefully it shouldn't take too long, or you could find yourself losing a lot of commission! As an accountable, professional salesperson, it's your duty to do this in order to give the best service possible by being your true self. Engaging in arguments and long debates will not get the job moving forward and will never end with a positive outcome. You'll only end up in emotional distress and ruin your frequency, making it harder to sell. Never let these negative people enter your world, as they'll drag you down and beat you with experience. If they're a reasonable person they'll see your position and relent, if they aren't, acknowledge them for who they are and alter your future behavior to suit. You must figuratively fight for your sales, but don't expect miracles, especially if you're dealing with somebody who's unreasonable. It's your job as a professional to adapt your approach and not put yourself in a position where you interact with such people on a regular basis. If you've gained respect on the shop floor, you might be surprised at what happens when you challenge somebody about a sale.

I heard a saying a while back that resonates with this scenario: "You can either be right or you can be successful."

It's your job to look after your own emotional wellbeing, nobody else's, so do what's right for you. You need to gain the respect of your colleagues, but you won't do this by submitting to their will just because there is a little pressure. In sales, there will always be pressure, and depending on the environment you're in, some floors will be more aggressive than others. This doesn't mean you act in an aggressive way; it means you expand your emotional awareness to accept what's going on and maneuver around it. Start to accept other people for who they are rather than judging them or fighting their characteristics. This will cause less strain on your emotional wellbeing and leave you more focused to sell.

Just because you're working with somebody doesn't mean you're obligated to speak to them, especially if they're negative. Once you see them for who they are, acknowledge that and interact with them differently in the future. You're working in a professional setting and as long as it remains professional, that will suffice. You aren't at work to find friends. If a toxic colleague says something negative to you, even if it's just a trivial matter such as how they had a bad evening or are not happy to be back at work, don't feel the need to fully acknowledge it or take it on board. It's your priority to protect your own frequency and not let others bring you down. It's not your job to sort all the problems of others as they're on their own life journey.

Grey rocking and giving vague or one-word answers to people who rock your frequency is essential to protecting your emotional wellbeing, either at work or indeed out of work. This is similar to how you should tell a "white lie" to your managers and colleagues about a potential deal being made. Never let on or be too honest about a scenario or situation. Always hold a little back. If somebody does bait you to alter your frequency, give them the answer "yeah." This will stop them in their tracks and allow you to move forward with the job at hand.

If it's a genuine comment and a friend needs a word of advice, then of course you should assist and comfort your colleagues. Very often, when times were tough and no customers were walking through the door, people would be losing their minds and acting as if it was never going to be busy again. More often than not, I was the one who told them, "It'll come when it comes," and to stay strong and ready for the customers when they come in. Not only did this help my colleagues, but it also helped the customers. Nobody wants to be served by an anxious, needy salesperson, like we've stated in the chapters before. If they tend to be manipulative, however, I would stay well clear of these situations and look after your emotional welfare. As you become more self-aware and your emotional intelligence increases, you'll start to realize what's bait and what isn't.

Never lower your frequency to fit in with colleagues. Either allow them to raise their level to yours or leave them behind. There is no other option if you want to be successful.

Be there for your reasonable colleagues and make them feel better by having conversations and cracking jokes to help take the stress away from them. Not because you feel you should do it out of duty, but because you want to do it. It will make them and you feel better, plus the shop floor will be more harmonious too, which is exactly what customers need when they walk through the door. Having great camaraderie on a shop floor is an awesome feeling, especially when serving customers, as there's an almost telepathic understanding between colleagues. There is no greater experience than working on a team that supports each other, writes orders up for each other, and has one another's back. Always strive for this working relationship with your colleagues wherever possible. You'll book more business and have happier customers in the process. Every working relationship is different, but you always need to assert yourself if you genuinely feel that you have been aggrieved. If you don't, you'll only end up being walked all over.

Who's serving who and the commission can come into question in many ways. Perhaps a colleague doesn't know you're serving somebody; perhaps they do, and they're trying their luck. Perhaps you're serving a customer they served in the past. Regardless of the amount, I would never let another sales professional write up an order of mine. It could be a $50 item that wouldn't make or break my week, but that isn't the point. I'd served the customer and wanted to see the order through until the end.

Customers also prefer this continuity of one person serving them, which adds to their experience. When one person is the face of their transaction, they call you up and ask for you by name, as they have a relationship with you. This could be for bad news, such as service complaints or issues, but it could also be for nicer subjects, such as repeat business and referrals.

Other salespeople are addicted to behavioral patterns because they're an easy excuse for why they're not performing the way they should. These are excuses such as, "Oh, it's such-and-such's fault that I haven't hit my target," or "If this happened, then that would have happened, and I would have hit my period." These are statements and emotional responses that are ingrained in some salespeople's minds. Those attitudes help them escape from the fact that they were wrong, are not as sharp as they could have been, haven't learned from past experiences, and/or didn't do something different to alter their results.

The moment a salesperson looks at themselves as the catalyst for why a particular scenario didn't play out the way they wanted, they're winning. This level of acceptance is great and sets the foundation for true growth, as hard as it is to endure in the short term.

Have the humility to ask yourself why a particular "bad" scenario is playing out. Is there a lesson you need to be taught? Have you got to tailor your approach to lower sales resistance? Are you too flustered and rushing people into decisions? Do you need to ground yourself in order to be more confident and assertive? By asking this until you are in full "sales swing," you will keep refining your approach until you become a master salesperson.

Once somebody has wronged you for their own gain instead of doing the right thing, the chances are there's no going back since the trust is broken. This may seem rather black and white, but people very rarely change. If somebody does show true remorse, then give the relationship another shot. If, however, you're hearing the same old sob story after they've wronged you, remember how many times you've heard it before. At some point, you need to realize it's your fault you keep engaging in these relationships, and it's your attitude that has to change.

It's very easy to be misled or let your mind wander when in a busy store, as there are millions of things happening at once, but this is where living a cleaner and more mindful life will help. When you're coming into work as sharp as a new pin and have the intention of looking after yourself emotionally, keeping negative scenarios and people away from you, and doing your best, nothing will get past you. You'll remember the frequency you need to be on and who, what, and where to avoid to remain on it.

Many times, I have lost my head, either outside of work or even at work, only to fall back into a toxic relationship and lose all the hard work of creating the sales momentum that allowed me to become the top performer. Only when I remembered that some people were interacting with me for their own gain and that I had to stand on my own two feet away from the crowd, was I able to channel my focus into the momentum needed to be number one. These are the acts of a leader, and it is very rare to see a leader losing their mind or throwing a temper tantrum because of scenarios that are happening around them. Contain these emotions at all times. People may be angry or triggered by the fact that you're starting to be your true, confident, contained self, but none of that matters as long as you're doing what is best for you and your family's future. Everybody on the shop floor, including customers, will look to you as a leader, and therefore you'll be the go-to guy or gal to help them with their purchase.

This new-found gravitas from all the work you've been putting in will also be noticed by your colleagues. The issue here could be that the original go-to guy or gal won't like it, but that's their problem, not yours, so stay strong and positive. As long as you stick to the ground rules of the store, you cannot be painted as the bad guy or scapegoated. By the same token, be aware that not everybody else has the same principles, and if somebody is pushing the limits of these principles, boundaries must be created.

> *"If you can keep your head when all about*
> *you are losing theirs and blaming it on*
> *you..." - Rudyard Kipling*

For the ideal customer experience, a sales professional can't serve more than three customers at once. I've tried more but have been spread way too thin and never given the service that was required. This is why having guidelines in place is so important in a workplace for two reasons: 1) it's not just a free for all, and 2) every customer is served to the same high standard.

Even if there were customers waiting to be served, I wouldn't enter into sales-related interactions with them. As far as I was concerned, the rule was the rule, and I had my own ethical and moral code to stick to too. It's a manager's job to manage the shop floor and ensure that all customers are being served and tended to correctly. Customers have even said to me that they just needed a salesperson because they were buying a certain product and wanted me to serve them. Some would have been almost throwing their wallets at me to take the order, but I'd find a manager to serve them after explaining that I was tied up at the minute, or other words to that effect, even though it killed me inside.

This may sound ludicrous, but it kept my frequency in check and my conscience clear. Also, it gave no opportunity for backbiting and kept the high standard I was working toward when it came to leading by example. The amount of commission I have had to give up in this way is frightening just because I kept to my moral code in the short term, but in reality, I believe I gained more by doing so. I kept to my principles, and because of that, my energy and momentum flowed. If I had caved and taken the easy money, my frequency and emotional state would have spiked. Chances were, the other customers who I was serving would have picked up on that and not bought, or at a very minimum, would have been in a different level of rapport that wasn't as strong. As we know by now, this will kill a long-term sales relationship.

When people are under pressure, their true colors will show for what they are, and this is where true leaders are either created or fall by the wayside. Never trust other people's opinions about other individuals; always be wary and make your own judgment, regardless of how much peer pressure there is.

Gaslighting, smear campaigns, trying to have a joke with you so you hopefully forget the scenario (buying you gifts or making drinks is always a winner here), or perhaps even pure intimidation. These are all behaviors that you could and probably will experience when climbing through the ranks and increasing your quota. Yes, it's hard to tolerate, but I implore you to be strong and avoid succumbing to negative behaviors.

You must be mentally prepared for the drama when it does unfold, so it doesn't catch you off guard. This does not mean that you go looking for conflict with your colleagues. Remember your emotional battery? Once you see patterns in people's behavior, you'll become better at navigating them.

Never react emotionally as you'll lose the likelihood of influencing the sale and situation. This could be something like getting angry, upset, or sometimes even genuinely laughing. Any emotional reaction that makes your contained enthusiasm spill over will ruin your peace of mind and focus. Keep that momentum bubbling away.

It takes 100% of your focus to inspire people enough to buy from you, any less than this and they won't. If somebody has done or said something that's knocked you off your game, pause for a second and collect yourself before speaking to your customer to get back into the frequency that's needed. Take the time to clear your mind, be at peace in the setting you're in. In sales, you must be prepared to not care what others think of you in order to be successful and inspire others to buy. Never act in a hot-headed manner and take your frustration out on the customer; you'll only burn the sale and the relationship and lose your self-respect in the process.

So many times, I have literally stopped in my tracks to compose my emotions and clear my mind before interacting with a customer. I have literally walked to find an area in the store where there was distance from the drama that was unfolding to compose my emotions before talking to them. This may sound strange and could have looked even stranger, but I didn't care. It helped me take ownership of my emotions, feelings, and thoughts, which enabled me to interact with the customer in a manner they deserved and gave me the highest likelihood of gaining the sale.

> *"Those who have swords and know how to use them but keep them sheathed will inherit the world" - Jordan Peterson.*

Gary Vaynerchuk summed it up perfectly in this quote about building the biggest building in town, "To do this you do one of two things. You either build the biggest building in town, or you try your best to tear down all the other buildings."

The best revenge you can ever have isn't trying to bring them down; it's outperforming them. As you stop engaging in politics and start being your best sales self, after a few short weeks, the pressure will start to slow down as people realize this new behavior isn't just an attitude change; it's a complete behavioral change.

Many times, I have sensed that someone's energy conflicts with my own on a shop floor, or indeed, in the wide world. I literally stepped out of their space to create my own. This could be a slight sideways step or even moving to another side of the store. This allows me to "step out" of their world and create my own. From then on, I became comfortable being present with myself and my surroundings, and this created a new energy that people were attracted to.

Over time, as you have changed, your people will gravitate towards your natural energy, and you'll stop entering into drama, arguments, or politics.

You must be willing to stand on your own and not care what others think. I've been called a loner and all kinds of other names because of my behaviors. Did I care? No. I was at the top, earning more money than them, and being my true self.

If you're feeling resistance in your body or that you're having to force things to "make" them happen, take stock of what's going on around you. Have you got to change your approach? Are you entering into other people's energies? Be responsible enough to be in charge of your own actions rather than being led by others.

As the dust starts to settle, the atmosphere will be slightly different. If this is the case, never think that people have changed their ways just because you've changed yours. Ensure you're on your a-game at all times or the same people will realise this and look to take advantage. In fact, it was you that made your own life difficult by not being as sharp as you could have been. This is tricky as you're working in extremely close proximity to each other, but this is a part of the job and being professional. If you make a mistake that jeopardizes your position, accept that you have and learn from it.

Mistakes could be acting on impulse and serving a customer that wasn't yours to serve, letting somebody you know isn't good for you back into your psyche, or saying something you regret. This is all a part of life, and as long as you learn from your mistakes, you'll be a better person for it. Sometimes customers may ask you questions about a product when another sales consultant is meant to be serving them. This can be extremely annoying as you aren't getting paid for the work that you're doing, but unfortunately it happens, and as you're representing the same company, certain standards must be met. Answer the question that they've asked out of courtesy, and then proceed to tell the said professional that they're asking questions, accept that the interaction is over, and leave them to it. These are examples of shop floor politics that you and your company have decided on. Whatever you decide, you must stick with it, or you'll create animosity within the team.

Don't let your emotions overflow because of how upset answering questions for other people's customers has made you. It's part and parcel of the job, and you must be able to deal with it and then get back into your sales frequency. If the professional isn't interested or sharp enough to be aware of his or her surroundings, mention to a manager how they aren't pulling their weight and how it's having an impact on your job. The same goes if a colleague walks around the floor serving everybody without having any respect for their colleagues. Although, first, I would advise you to try to handle the situation on your own before raising the issue.

I remember a story I was told about a salesman who never respected other colleagues and thought that each customer was his and nobody else's. One day, two customers came walking into the store; he served one, leaving the other to be served by another salesperson. When the other salesperson served the customer, they found out that it was a service issue rather than a potential sale and had to deal with the problem. When the salesperson loaded the order on the computer, they looked to see whose order it originally was. Yep, you guessed it. The one that had completely ignored them and went for the fresh customer!

The salesperson who was serving the service issue politely said to the customer that they would go fetch the original salesperson to deal with them as they would have had a stronger relationship and may even know more about the finer details than them. When the salesperson delivered the news, their colleague apparently went ballistic and exclaimed how they were childish and petty. I'm not saying I completely agree with the salesperson who chose to fetch the original salesperson to deal with the service issue because there is a point to taking ownership and doing the right thing. However, I also see the point that this was a golden opportunity to get back at the unruly colleague who thought he was being clever and was above everybody else.

Personally, whenever a scenario like this comes up, I always try to rise above it and remember that a certain person can't be trusted and to keep them at arms' length. If it gets to the point that it's too uncomfortable to work in, raise an issue or find new employment. This isn't weakness; being the better person and walking away is an act of strength.

In sales, you should not only be two steps ahead of your customers; if you want to be at the top, you must be two steps ahead of your colleagues too. Even if you may lose a sale in the short term, always think of the big picture treat every scenario, relationship, or interaction as an experience, and look for what you can learn from it.

A little paranoia in sales is fantastic to stay sharp and competitive. Learning the methods that your colleagues use will help you succeed. Always figuratively looking over your shoulder in sales is essential, especially given its relentless nature. There will always be somebody who is looking to seize an opportunity either ethically or unethically, and you should always be aware of that. You must be streetwise enough in your approach and learn from your mistakes to maintain momentum, because as soon as it leaves you, it's an uphill battle to get it going again.

If another salesperson has made a mistake and is speaking to customers that you're serving, or perhaps a customer has asked them for help even if you're on hand to answer (that does happen), simply let them know with a polite wave or when there is a break in the conversation. Most people will play fair, but if not and the problem keeps happening, speak to a manager to discuss it.

Take an independent stance and try your best to sort out your own issues first without running to a manager every time a little issue occurs, or you'll lose your self-respect. It's similar to going home every night and complaining to your wife about something that keeps bothering you. Sooner or later, if you don't step up to sort it yourself, she'll leave you. There has got to be a front that says nothing bothers you in order to gain the respect and credibility you need to be seen as a leader. The second you start focusing on the negative, that's where your energy will flow. You'd be surprised how receptive people are if you first instigate a conversation to move relationships forward, but remember to stick to your principles.

If you do discuss this with your line manager because issues can't be resolved and they act passively or, even worse, add fuel to the flames, I suggest you prepare to exit and leave your place of work. This may sound extreme, but working in a toxic workplace isn't productive and isn't good for your personal growth. As you're focused on your mission to be the best salesperson you can be, you may be described as ruthless or cold, but this is all irrelevant. As long as you stay strong, focused, and act in a moral manner while serving customers correctly, who is anybody else to criticize your methods?

Others may say that this is taking work too seriously and that there should be room for playful teasing or banter, but people perceive humor in different ways, and it's very easy to border on passive aggressiveness. I would advise you not to engage in these tactics and to keep your mind present and on the job at hand. You'll earn more money for yourself and your family and provide a better service by doing so.

There is a saying in England that apparently the Royal Family uses that goes, "Never complain. Never explain." I love the principle. Never complaining about anything that happens to you, within reason, will keep you positive, disciplined, and at the correct frequency for customers to relate to you easier and quicker. Never explain your actions to somebody else, as long as they're moral, ethical, and stick within the guidelines. It's your business you're running, remember? If you owned a flower shop and made a business decision to put another flower shop owner's nose out of joint, would you backtrack or would you carry on regardless?

If a manager asks you to justify, then I suppose that's reason enough as sometimes you may act out of alignment with the rulings. In this case you can refine your approach to be better for next time.

You may think that there is safety in numbers, i.e., the team on the floor, but you aren't going to get number one or even reach part of your potential if you're just following the pack. This means not going along with the status quo and fitting in just because it's easier to do so, rather than putting it all on the line. It may be tricky at first, as it's very easy for people to stand in a crowd and make remarks rather than being their authentic selves. Make sure you rise above these scenarios, as they won't last forever. Keep your emotions in check and your frequency high, and you'll work through it.

Something always comes up if you stay positive.

> *"The brighter you shine, the more shadows you will cast." - She Heng Yi.*

So many people need to have the feeling of being liked by other people, but this won't propel you to where you need to be. Especially if the ones you're trying to get the approval of aren't the ones that have your best interests at heart. Be the one that is misunderstood by others; if you're not misunderstood, then you're not different, and you certainly won't be at the top by just fitting in.

Learn to accept that what's happening around you isn't personal; people's behavior reflects others'. Surrender to your surroundings, like surrendering to serving customers, and accept the environment you're in. This doesn't mean you act as a wet blanket, but by surrendering, you aren't in resistance and are able to compensate and roll with the punches.

I remember watching an interview with a CEO on TV when I was a child. The CEO mentioned how he spoke with a therapist who told him to be more like a palm tree swaying in the storm rather than trying to beat the weather by standing tall and rigid.

> *"Men are born soft and supple; dead, they are stiff and hard. Plants are born tender and pliable; dead, they are brittle and dry. Thus, whoever is stiff and inflexible is a disciple of death. Whoever is soft and yielding is a disciple of life."* - Lao Tzu

I used to, and still do, love to serve customers and help them find the product of their dreams. I always kept my faith that I could add value and change their lives with the product and service I gave, and this energy was transferred. I made a conscious choice to feel these emotions, and this elevated my frequency. It cast all negative ones aside and threw me into a state that would draw people in and open them up almost at will.

Customers love to be involved and served by people like this, as they have an air of grace about their presence. Others seem to be rushing around in a frazzled state while you're floating around the floor, interacting with customers at will. Of course, you're working hard to maintain this composure, and you still must put in the work, but the perception is that you have everything under control. It'll take time, but the easier things get, the more attractive you'll become, and people will be even more drawn to your presence.

Ever notice when you're on fire and customers seem to be buying from you left, right, and center? This is because of the momentum you've created; the trick is to keep this going at all times, even when there aren't customers to be served. Stay away from toxic situations or behaviors.

This is the difference between being average and being great. Greats don't care about politics or shop floor BS. They know it's part and parcel of the career they've chosen and don't care about what other people think. They aren't people pleasers who have to submit to every demand. You'll never live your best life this way. Sure, you'll fit in, but you won't be happy, and this is why you must be willing to do the difficult things.

This is all what Ed Mylett calls "compounding pounding." All of these 1% keep adding up, and over the space of a week, a month, or a year, you're miles ahead of everybody else. Whenever there was downtime and no customers in the store, I'd call leads that I'd taken or try to drum up extra business rather than standing around gossiping with other people. This created a sales funnel that helped keep momentum and energy flowing throughout the day.

There is always something to do in any setting, but it's about making the choice to do it rather than standing or sitting idle and gossiping. Whenever I'm going through a hard or stressful patch, I always serve unconditionally, and that brings me back into the correct frequency to win.

Even when working with people you don't necessarily get along with, there's always something you can learn from them. They may have a certain quirk that works extremely well; they may use a certain phrase that allows customers to open up with ease; or they may use the way they handle their body language to persuade others. Getting to number one isn't about being ignorant of the world around you and plowing headfirst into the task. Sometimes it pays dividends to take a look at the world and see what others are doing, then decide what works well and what doesn't. I suppose that's the reason you're reading this book!

Everywhere I have worked, it has always been a free-for-all system. This means that when a customer walks through the door, you serve them in no particular order. As a gentleman's agreement, I would always meet and greet one customer while leaving the next customer that would enter the store to other consultants, provided there were others available. If, for instance, another consultant wasn't too bothered about serving them, or they were perhaps on their mobile phone at the back of the store, by all means I'd be all over those customers in the same manner.

I did this for two reasons. The first is that it's fair for the customer, and the second is that you're giving everybody else a chance. Everybody needs to have an equal opportunity to earn money and have a fair crack at whatever comes through the door, and therefore you must have the grace to give them that chance. I know that's hard to accept, but it's true. Not every consultant will be like this, as some are hungrier than others, and in these scenarios, you need to be ready for any customers that come into the store from the moment you walk through the door. As said in one of the first chapters, you're already in this state of mind, so it shouldn't be an issue.

Not everybody will live by these rules, but that's up to them. Some retailers work on a numbered system. Accept that's the way they are and move around them.

The only way this would be effective is if there is a strong, fair manager who manages the floor correctly. Salespeople will have their heads down serving customers and won't have the capacity to look at who else is coming through the door, especially if they're serving two to three customers at a time. If you can't tie a customer down with a deposit and they come in at a later date, you need to be extra vigilant about who's coming through the door. If not, opportunities will be missed, and you'll only have yourself to blame.

There are some companies that operate a "pen to pad" system. That basically means that customers are "free" right up until the point of them purchasing a product or service. This is wrong, as somebody could have spent hours with them only for them to decide a few hours later, and a sharky salesperson would write up the order and take the commission.

There has to be some sort of mutual respect between staff that will help ease the environment and atmosphere within the store. It doesn't mean that you can go around serving other people knowing that your order is safe while in the hands of somebody else, as this would be taking the liberty of their time. As a professional salesperson, it's your duty to see the job through, and you should have enough self-respect and dignity to do so. It's also your moral obligation to ensure that the customer is served to the best of your ability.

Never ignore a customer who looks to only be buying a smaller ticket item rather than a higher ticket one. Not only is this unfair to the customer, but it will kill your momentum. Always looking for the next best thing will only put you at a lower frequency instead of living in the present moment and accepting what is. You'll have a greater sense of satisfaction knowing that you're willing to put in the work for the smaller items as well as the bigger ones.

Never show any less focus or attention to these kinds of customers. Even if they're buying an item that's not going to make or break your target, they're still spending their hard-earned money and need to be treated as such. Just because somebody isn't spending thousands of dollars with you today doesn't mean that they won't in the future. If you ignore, offend, or act passively towards somebody just because of that smaller item, they aren't going to come to you a few months down the line when they're potentially purchasing the higher-ticket item. Always play the long game of sales and generate a relationship that will last forever. They may not purchase that big-ticket item from you, but there is always that possibility, so never burn a bridge of opportunity.

Repeat customers will sniff out this behavior over time, as they're people with feelings and they'll remember what happened to them before. I've seen it many times. Always be that constant source of strength, regardless of the situation. It's very often the smaller sales that will project you onto the bigger ones, as these can create confidence when times may start to get tough. However, if you have a choice between serving two customers, one of whom is a high-ticket sale and the other is not, always go for the higher ticket. It goes without saying, right?

I remember once serving a couple who were looking at a coffee table. Everybody ignored the pair. I served them like anybody else and spoke quite in depth about why it was a good fit for them, how it would suit the room, and the benefits they would receive from it.

They then chose to buy the table but also added a few more items to the bill, such as the table lamp, the rug, the three-seater, and the two-seater I was sitting on. A $300 coffee table all of a sudden turned into a $4,000 order. Sure, these don't happen very often, but they happen, so never judge somebody or their purchases.

Side note: Never purposely sabotage or steal commission from others, as this will only lower your frequency. I've been there, thinking I'd get somebody back and take revenge for an order that I lost, but it rarely ever worked out. In most cases, it actually backfired on me. Again, you'll only lower your standing and self-respect.

Bringing it All Together

Hopefully, now you've learned how to be a top salesperson without being slimy or hard-nosed. By putting these skills and methods into practice, you'll certainly strengthen sales relationships with your customers and be on your way to double your sales with half the stress in two years or less. Guaranteed. Let's go over some of the key points that should be applied in order to be the top salesperson:

- Get an early night's sleep.

- Visualize your success.

- Don't engage in self-sabotaging behaviors.

- Keep your enthusiasm contained and bubbling away.

- Do the little things right, and the big things will take care of themselves.

- Be emotionally intelligent.

- Be accountable and responsible for your own actions.

- Don't enter into other people's negative emotions or vibes.

- Dress up.

- Slow down.

- Correct your body language and mindset.

- "Hi guys. Are you just looking, or are you looking for something in particular?"

- Take your time; never rush a customer.
- Don't BS them just to build rapport; let your actions do the talking.
- Actively listening is the biggest compliment you can give.
- Seek respect, not love.
- Come into the buyer's world at their frequency.
- Serve unconditionally.
- Stay positive.
- Be agreeable.
- Have the ability to ignore.
- Get the answer you want while enabling the customer to say "no."
- Never show more than three products to stay in a position of authority.
- Never let customers buy the first product they see (just yet).
- Challenge a customer's ideas in a loving, sincere, and caring way.
- Pro-actively overcome objections like a champ.
- Remain "neutral" and detach yourself from the sale.
- Stay cool and logical rather than emotional during objection handling and negotiation.
- Address the hesitation of the customer BEFORE closing.

- Always ask for the order.

- Show appreciation and thank the customer.

- Provide referral letters to entice customers to recommend you.

- Bundle your products and services to make the buying experience easy and seamless.

- Use strategic alliances and partnerships to build your client base and treat them as VIPs!

- Never try to be manipulative, underhanded, or deceptive; it only raises resistance.

- Never be too pushy or desperate; always play the long game of sales to reduce sales resistance.

- Keep it simple.

- Happy people sell more.

Which one is your favorite? Maybe I've missed one? If you can implement even half of these skills, you're well on your way to becoming the top performer in your store and increasing your commission dramatically.

Every year I take a select few students and help them Double Your Sales With Half The Stress In 2 Years Or Less, Guaranteed. Seventy-five percent of the fee is linked to results. Fair enough?

If you'd like to apply, see if you'd be a good fit. Contact me by the means below:

info@fromfeartomindful.com

www.linkedin.com/in/sam-king-from-fear-to-mindful/

I also offer a great referral incentive to anyone who refers a salesperson or company that may benefit from this program and gets through the application process.

Writing this book has been both one of the hardest and one of the best experiences I have ever had. Thank you so much for taking the time to read this and being a part of it.

Please give this book a review on the website that you bought it from. Include a selfie of you and the book in your favorite reading spot too!

I'd love to know how you implemented these strategies and the impact they had on your business. Let me know using the means below!

info@fromfeartomindful.com

www.linkedin.com/in/sam-king-from-fear-to-mindful/

www.fromfeartomindful.com

I can't wait to work with you soon.